Pilgrim Progression

09

The Religious Contours of California
Window to the World's Religions

A nine-volume series co-edited by
Phillip E. Hammond and Ninian Smart
DEPARTMENT OF RELIGIOUS STUDIES
UNIVERSITY OF CALIFORNIA, SANTA BARBARA

VOLUME I
Californian Catholicism
KAY ALEXANDER

VOLUME II
Pilgrim Progression: *The Protestant Experience in California*
ELDON G. ERNST AND DOUGLAS FIRTH ANDERSON

VOLUME III
Competing Visions of Paradise:
The California Experience of 19th Century American Sectarianism
JOHN K. SIMMONS AND BRIAN WILSON

VOLUME IV
Diaspora in a Golden Land:
The Judaisms of California
RICHARD D. HECHT,
WITH RICHARD L. HOCH AND AVA G. KAHN

FORTHCOMING BOOKS ON:
Native American Religions
East Asian Religions
Islam
New Religious Movements
South Asian Religions

Pilgrim Progression
The Protestant Experience in California

ELDON G. ERNST

with DOUGLAS FIRTH ANDERSON

VOLUME II OF
The Religious Contours of California
Window to the World's Religions

A PROJECT OF
The Center for the Study of Religion
University of California, Santa Barbara

IN ASSOCIATION WITH
The California Historical Society

FITHIAN PRESS
SANTA BARBARA • 1993

Copyright © 1993 by the Regents of the University of California

Design and typography by Jim Cook

Published by Fithian Press
Post Office Box 1525
Santa Barbara, California 93102

LIBRARY OF CONGRESS CATALOGING-IN-PUBLICATION DATA
Ernst, Eldon G.
    Pilgrim progression: the Protestant experience in California /
Eldon G. Ernst, with Douglas Firth Anderson.
    p.   cm. — (The Religious contours of California; v. 2)
    Includes bibliographical references and index.
    ISBN 1-56747-063-3
    1. Protestant churches—California—History. 2. California—
Church history. I. Anderson, Douglas Firth. II. Title. III. Series.
BR555.C2E76   1993
280'.4'09794—dc20   93-14626
                                                              CIP

Contents

The Religious Contours
of California

The series of books of which this volume is part is meant to engage the interest of California's citizens in the religions of their state. These range from Christian groups to Muslims, from Jews to Buddhists. They include the religions of Native Americans, of East Asian immigrants, and varieties of African American faith. The "new" religious movements of the 1960s and '70s are well represented in this state, as well as religions born in nineteenth-century America, such as Mormonism and Christian Science, and they too are part of this series. California, as is well known, is a heterogeneous society, and its religious life is likewise diverse; our series reveals just how diverse.

The series has a second purpose, however, and that is to inform readers about the world's religions. It is one thing to learn, for example, about Islam, Judaism, or Christianity as they have been and are practiced in California; it is another thing to discover where such religions originated, how they developed, and where else they currently are found. Each volume in the series therefore fits, at least loosely, a common outline. Each begins with an introduction to some religious tradition as it is found in California, then moves to an analysis of the interplay of that tradition and the state: how is California affected by the presence of this tradition, and how is the tradition affected by its presence in California? It is during this analysis that the reader learns about the history and global experience of the religious tradition that is the book's focus, for in attempting to understand any spiritual tradition in California one necessarily compares the situation here with situations elsewhere. The series will be successful, then, to the degree readers find they have learned not only about a religion close at hand, but learned also about that religion worldwide.

The series arose out of a project pioneered at the University of California at Santa Barbara to help high school teachers and others understand world religions through their manifestations in California. We conceived the parallel idea of recruiting a team of authors who would be able to put together a lucid set of books to inform the general public of the ways in which this state has drawn on divergent sources of religious belief and practice in forming a multicultural and rich society. In many ways California is indeed the future.

We believe that this series will help to fulfill one of the obligations of the University of California: to bring knowledge and understanding to the citizens of this great state, and to others in America, and to return directly some of the benefits conferred on us as researchers and teachers by its tax-paying citizens. Thus, royalties from the sales of these books go not to the authors or editors but into a fund the purpose of which is the furtherance of the public's understanding of all religious traditions. We hope we can in such a way make a small contribution to a fruitful living together of diverse spiritual practices.

In all this we try to be what may be called warmly objective. The authors, as students of religion, wish to give a fair and rounded account of each religion. We are not, as scholars of religions, in the business of preaching, of course, but we wish to bring out something of the spirit of each tradition. This series is thus a contribution to the mutual understanding of religions as well as a means of giving readers an idea of California's religious variety. We are grateful to the Lilly Endowment and to the Provost at UCSB for their financial assistance in publishing the series.

PHILLIP E. HAMMOND
NINIAN SMART
Editors

Acknowledgements

The Protestant experience in California is a complex and fascinating story that historians have not yet fully woven into the fabric of American religious history. Much credit is due to Phillip Hammond, Ninian Smart, and their colleagues at the University of California at Santa Barbara for their pioneering efforts to stimulate and help facilitate research and writing in California religious history, including this brief introduction to Protestantism.

The immediate context and resources for the writing of this volume were greatly enhanced by a generous grant from the Lilly Endowment to a team of scholars associated with the University of California at Santa Barbara and with the Graduate Theological Union in Berkeley studying "Region and Mainline Religion."

My awareness of the need to take account of religion in far western American history, and of the Far West in American religious history, has developed from my association with Harland Hogue in the Graduate Theological Union since 1967. To him I owe my original interest in the subject. His knowledge and enthusiasm about nineteenth-century California Protestantism has nurtured my teaching and scholarship over the years.

Over the past quarter century in the Graduate Theological Union I have been privileged to work closely with many fine graduate students in the field of American religious history. In their cultural orientations and in their chosen research topics they represent the Anglo-European, Asian-Pacific, African, Hispanic, and Native

9

American identities, plus the broad plurality of traditions that permeate California religious history. Among those whose programs I directed, several produced doctoral dissertations in specialized topics of California religious history: Larry G. Murphy, Wesley Woo, Catherine Ann Curry, P.V.V.M., Douglas Firth Anderson, Michael Lawrence Mickler, William Mead Muhler, and Ryo Yoshida. Their scholarship has contributed much to my understanding of topics covered in this volume, as have the studies of Michael E. Engh, S.J. and Richard Gribble, CSC, with whom I worked in their graduate programs.

Douglas Firth Anderson, now a member of the faculty of Northwestern College in Orange City, Iowa, was my student, colleague and collaborator in the field during the 1980s. He contributed significantly to the content of this volume, especially to chapters three and five (though I must accept responsibility for any inaccuracies or flawed interpretations that appear in the text). He and I appreciate the financial aid given to him by Northwestern College for travel to California during the summer of 1990, when portions of this book were planned and written.

Finally, I acknowledge four colleagues who in various ways have offered unusual support of my efforts to understand religion in far western United States history: Winthrop S. Hudson has been my mentor for over thirty years; John Baker-Batsel provided me with a context of access to library resources for my research; Ross Hidy has inspired me by his visionary and organizational leadership in the preservation of church archives of the North American Pacific regions; and Barbara Brown Zikmund has offered the kind of ongoing creative thinking, enthusiasm, and collegial friendship that has encouraged me to see the project through to the end.

—ELDON G. ERNST

1 California Protestant Panorama

In the year 1579, sailing for England's Protestant Queen Elizabeth, Sir Francis Drake with his company of adventurers landed on the Marin peninsula just north of San Francisco Bay. Included in the group was the Reverend Francis Fletcher, chaplain of the Church of England. They celebrated the first English Christian liturgy (rites for public worship) in North America, and they represented the first Protestant Christian presence in the region to be known as California.

But this was an isolated event. No English settlement in California resulted from Drake's landing, and no Christian church was planted. Although the English Protestant Pilgrims and Puritans were about to found their colonies at Jamestown, Virginia (1603), Plymouth, Massachusetts (1620), and other locations along the North American Atlantic seaboard, it would be well over two centuries before Christians of British or other northern European ancestry would settle in California on the Pacific Coast side of the continent.

By the time Anglo Protestants did begin to arrive in California, moreover, spurred by the discovery of gold at the end of the 1840s, two kinds of Christian settlements distinctively non-British or non-northern European had been established in California. Twenty-one Spanish Roman Catholic missions had been planted up the coast from San Diego to Sonoma (1769-1824), and a Russian Orthodox chapel had been built in 1824 at Fort Ross near Bodega Bay (near the spot of Drake's landing). Despite their head start in the area, however, neither the Catholics nor the Russian Orthodox sustained much church activity into the 1840s. The missions had been allowed to deteriorate, and the Russians had relinquished their foothold by the time of the Gold Rush. With the coming of the '49ers, therefore—and Protestantism with them—a whole new chapter in California history began, introducing an unprecedented mixture of ethnic and religious group identities.

People have been moving to California in great waves since it became a state in 1850. Coming from nations near and far, as well as from other parts of the United States, they have brought the world's ethnic cultures and religions to California. Among them have been Protestants calling themselves Methodists, Baptists, Congregationalists, Episcopalians, Presbyterians, Unitarians, Lutherans, Quakers, Disciples of Christ, Mennonites, Nazarenes, Assemblies of God, and a host of other church names. Many have added other labels, such as evangelicals, confessionalists, modernists, fundamentalists, social gospelers, charismatics, ecumenists, neo-orthodox, and so forth. There have been Anglo- and Euro-American churches, Afro- and Asian-American churches, Hispanic and Native American Indian churches. In short, all kinds of Protestants from the nations of the world have settled and built churches in California, and for nearly a century and a half they have contributed to the state's mixture of religious cultures.

Who are these Californians called Protestants? Where are they located within the history of Christianity? How do they fit into the overall configuration of religious groups in California?

Identifying Protestant Californians

Protestant Californians represent varieties of one of the three major historic expressions of Christianity as a world religion (the other two being Roman Catholicism and Eastern Orthodoxy).

A World Christian Movement

Protestantism is identified, first, as a *major* expression of *world* Christianity because it exists among large numbers of people in most nations on all continents. Among the 1.5 billion or so Christians worldwide, in 1980 Protestants numbered well over 300 million, nearly 3 million of them (close to 1 percent) residing in California.

Second, Protestants are distinguished by their seemingly unbridled tendency to increase their distinctive *varieties*. Whereas Roman Catholics of all kinds are united under the Roman Pope, and the various nationally-organized Eastern Orthodox Churches are united in a "holy tradition" (inherited beliefs, customs, and practices), Protestant diversity has thrived in ever-increasing numbers of essentially autonomous bodies expressing a plurality of traditions. Consequently a majority of the world's more than 20,000 independent Christian groups may be classified as Protestant. In California there are at least 75 separate denominations (organized bodies of churches), plus many more independent local churches and other kinds of Protestant organizations.

Third, the many varieties of Protestants represent a worldwide *movement* of Christians who share a particular sense of *historic* identity. That identity is rooted in the sixteenth-century Reformation in western Europe and Britain when western Catholic Christianity (in distinction from Eastern Orthodoxy) divided into the Roman Catholic Church on the one hand, and several new kinds of Protestant churches on the other hand. Protestants (protesters, advocates), stimulated by such leaders as Martin Luther, Menno Simons, Faustus Socinus, John Calvin, John Knox, and Richard Hooker, were among those attempting to reform the church from what they perceived to be long-developing corruptions in its teachings, practices, and organization. The Protestants opposed, and finally were separated from, the power and authority of the Roman Bishop (the pope) and formed new Christian groups independent of the Roman Catholic Church. Lutheran churches, Reformed churches, Mennonite churches, the Church of England (Episcopalians), and the early seventeenth-century Puritan churches (those dissenting from the Church of England—Presbyterians, Congregationalists, Baptists, and Quakers) became new Protestant traditions with their own creeds and confessions, worship forms, and structures of leadership and government. The list of new Protestant groups would continue to grow during the centuries following.

By the time Protestants began settling in California some 300 years later, their connections to these sixteenth-century European roots had become obscured by the distance of time, geography, and cultural identities. For many those roots were indirect and mixed. Methodists, for example, traced their denominational origins within Anglicanism (the Church of England) to the eighteenth-century spiritual awakening in Europe and America; while the Disciples of Christ traced theirs to the nineteenth-century American frontier. Furthermore, African, Asian, and Native American Protestants mixed their distinctively non-European cultural heritages with Reformation-rooted Christianity.

In the fullest sense, therefore, to identify California Protestants we must take account of the worldwide European explorations and colonial expansion that began about the time of the Reformation, reaching a peak during the nineteenth century. Protestants were part of this movement. Everywhere they went, European Protestants established new churches along national and ethnic lines. Often indigenous (native-born) churches began out of this contact with Protestantism, and just as often new churches were formed when Protestants differed over matters of particular beliefs and practices. Diversifying into new independent bodies, therefore, is a continual element in Protestants' historical experience and a mark of their identity as a world religious movement.

Protestantism is a distinctive world religion precisely because it did expand outside of western Europe and was able to assimilate into many cultures and express itself in many varieties. But it also is distinctive because wherever it went it carried elements of its sixteenth-century Reformation origins, giving them ever new flavors of expression at different times and places—including California.

Therefore we might identify Protestant Californians most broadly as *non-Roman Catholic Christians who trace their religious heritage, however remotely or indirectly, to sixteenth-century western Europe.* However distant and ambiguous the sixteenth-century Reformation may seem to many today, it represents a significant point of historical reference—the touchstone of a cluster of living traditions—that helps define Protestantism in all of its diversity.

The Reformation Traditions

On Sunday, October 23, 1983, at the Roman Catholic St. Mary's Cathedral in San Francisco, a spectacular ecumenical (worldwide Christian unity) celebration of music, word, and prayer commemorated the 500th birthday of the great Protestant reformer, Martin Luther. Leaders of the Episcopal (Anglican), Baptist, Methodist, Presbyterian, Congregational, and Lutheran denominational traditions took part in the service that was opened by the Roman Catholic Archbishop of San Francisco. Representatives from many denominations marched in the processional to the classic hymn written by Luther, "A Mighty Fortress Is Our God." The standing-room only congregation in the huge ultra-modern cathedral heard choral settings of melodies from the Greek Orthodox Service. "The word" was preached by Lutheran Krister Stendahl, eminent dean and professor of the New Testament at Harvard Divinity School. As the Congregation sang the recessional hymn, "Now Thank We All Our God," the participants filed out of the sanctuary in pairs, some wearing ecclesiastical robes, some not, to the reception held at the Lutheran Church just down the street.

Thus was the Reformation-rootage of Protestantism recognized by a broad panorama of Christian traditions living side-by-side in the predominantly Catholic City of Saint Francis by the Golden Gate.

The Protestant Reformation took place during the age of Renaissance in Europe (fourteenth to seventeenth centuries) that revived widespread interest in the arts and in classical Greco-Roman culture, including early Christianity. Rediscovering antiquity helped fuel the Reformation. The Protestant reformers were deeply interested in the origins and development of the early Christian churches in and around Palestine in the Near East where Jesus had lived and died, known today as "the holy land" to Jews, Christians, and Muslims alike. The early followers of Jesus proclaimed him to be "the Christ" (the expected Hebrew messiah, or saviour), and they became known as Christians. They formed communities for the purpose of worship, mutual support, and sharing the faith with others. Led by the apostle Paul, their mission moved beyond the Jewish people to the gentiles (non-Jews) and extended outside of Palestine in all directions of the Roman Empire. For three centuries they frequently were persecuted for their refusal to give supreme allegiance to the imperial gods, until the emperor Constantine proclaimed Christianity to be the official state religion early in the fourth century.

In various ways and degrees the first, sixteenth-century Protestants understood the church's reformation to be dependent upon recovering essential characteristics of "pre-Constantinian" Apostolic Christianity that they felt had been obscured in the developing traditions of medieval Christendom. They looked to the Bible to discover the original faith and expression of Christianity. In the New Testament they found early Christian accounts of the life of Jesus (the gospels of Matthew, Mark, Luke, and John), and of the early church's life and thought in, for example, the letters of Paul to the Romans, Corinthians, and other Christian communities. In the Old Testament they found the ancient heritage of Israel's faith in God with which Jesus and the early Christians identified. In these scriptures the Protestant reformers looked to the early Christians for guidance in reforming the doctrine (teaching), organization and leadership (polity), and practice (worship and moral life) of the church.

The reformers differed, however, in what they found to be *most* significant in Apostolic Christianity, and these differences contributed to the emergence of major Protestant denominational traditions. Thus, the most radical "restorationists" of New Testament Christianity were the Anabaptists, whose descendents became known as Mennonites, Hutterites, and Amish. Recalling the experience of the persecuted early Christians, they gathered into ordered communities withdrawn from the world of civil affairs. Less extreme was Martin Luther, who emphasized almost exclusively the need to recover the essential New Testament gospel (*evangel*— "good news") of God's saving grace in Jesus Christ for Christian theology and faith. The Lutheran (or Evangelical) tradition would distinguish sharply between the realm of the Gospel (the church's primary concern), and the realm of the civil order within which Christians must live their daily lives. In contrast, the architects of the Reformed Tradition, such as John Calvin and Huldreich Zwingli, were concerned to reform the church's organization and practices strictly according to New Testament patterns, while engaging the church in the reform of civil society as well. Though all were strongly influenced by this Reformed tradition, the English Protestant denominations distinguished themselves over issues of church government and relationships to the civil order. Episcopalians, Presbyterians, Congregationalists, Baptists, and Quakers each were convinced that their church organization and practices followed the New Testament pattern.

In time, all of these Protestant reform tendencies made their way to North America, and finally to California. Meanwhile, the process of reform continued to modify the traditions and create new ones. Time and again new reform movements, such as

Methodism, the Christian Movement (Disciples of Christ), the Adventist movement, the Holiness movement, and the Pentecostal movement would seek to recover what were perceived to be certain neglected New Testament patterns of Christianity.

The new Reformation traditions thus set in motion what has been called the "Protestant principle" of reform. Traditions—even the classic Reformation traditions—have been challenged, reshaped, and sometimes discarded as Protestantism has moved into new social-intellectual historical circumstances. This tendency to innovate finally so pluralized Protestantism that some of the traditions became reluctant to identify themselves as Protestant.

Most Unitarians, certain Anglicans, and some Baptists, for example, have shied away from the Protestant label when its modern identification seemed too broad or too narrow. Today it is not uncommon for some groups, concerned with traditions or expressions of belief and life styles, to question if others in fact are true Protestants or even Christians at all.

The importance of historic Christian tradition, therefore, always has been a major point of disagreement among Protestants. Compared with Roman Catholic Christians, for example, with whom they inherited traditions from the centuries of western European Christendom, Protestants generally have not identified as closely with or cared to preserve as much of the rich religious culture of the medieval church. Saints devotions, relics and icons, monastic orders, holy pilgrimages, the liturgical cycle of sacred days, and much of the sacramental practices of Catholic tradition to varying degrees were abandoned by most Protestant churches. Just how much to reject and retain of that long-developing tradition is an ongoing problem that has always divided Protestants and helps account for their major denominational differences. The Anglican Episcopal and Lutheran traditions, for example, have retained more of the medieval practices than have the more radical reform traditions such as Baptists and Mennonites. The Holiness and Pentecostal denominations, moreover, find the essence of Christian catholicity more in spiritual experience than in visible traditions.

Despite the occasional disclaimers by some Reformation-rooted traditions reluctant to identify with the whole Protestant spectrum, however, it would be historically inaccurate and confusing to abandon the name for them or them for the name. Beneath their real differences has been the common Protestant conviction that the early Apostolic Christians' faith and life were restored and therefore "reborn" in the spirit of the Reformation, and that this "rebirth" continues. Moreover, the Reformation spirit unleashed a cluster of priorities, emphases, and tendencies over which Protestants agree and differ, compete and cooperate; and these help us identify some common characteristics of the Protestant varieties that appeared as they moved from the Old World to the New World—and to California.

Protestant Characteristics

How, we might ask, can we recognize Protestant Californians when we see them?

First, we will discover manifestations of the independence and individuality that the Reformation had stamped indelibly on the entire Protestant movement. For example, we will notice recurring protests against real or threatened use of excessive power in church and state in religious matters, including Protestants resisting power of other Protestants. Especially in the American environment of Constitutional guarantee of religious freedom, Protestants have recognized no religious authority over either institutions or individuals other than what they have taken to be God's authority. They have asserted the freedom and responsibility of Christian persons and groups to think and act religiously according to their own consciences; and by so thinking and acting Protestants have divided at least as much as united, competed as much as cooperated on occasions of disagreement.

One particular doctrine almost universally held by Protestants since the Reformation illustrates the depth of this concern for freedom and responsibility in religious life and thought. This is the doctrine of "the priesthood of all believers," which means that all Christians, clergy and laity alike, are called to minister freely and responsibly to one another. The conviction underlying this doctrine is that all persons are essentially equal before God and that each individual has direct access to God without requiring a mediator of superior spiritual status. Regardless of how elaborate a clerical structure a Protestant denomination might have (a matter about which Protestants differ radically), the "common priesthood" principle remains. Moreover, the implications of this conviction are far reaching, influencing how Protestants understand the role of the Bible, the spirit, and the church in their religious life and thought.

Second, where there are Protestants, there will be the Bible. Protestants are exceptionally (sometimes fanatically) Bible-oriented. The Bible is the primary source of their understanding of Christian faith and life. For them the Bible somehow contains the "word of God"—the source of their knowledge of God's involvement in human history and of God's will for the quality of their own lives. Though they differ radically about the exact nature of biblical revelation, it is there that they seek the meaning, implications, and experience of "God's word." Consequently for Protestants the Bible takes authoritative precedence over the church, its tradition, its leaders, its worship forms and practices, its creeds and confessions. Though Protestants differ greatly in the significance they attach to these other aspects of their religious practice, few if any would rank them above the scriptures. Most important, however, is the Protestant conviction that the biblical revelation is accessible to all persons through their own reading, and consequently that all Christians should be encouraged to make studying the scriptures a central part of their spiritual life.

A third characteristic has to do with the spiritual life itself. In one way or another Protestants have tended to emphasize the importance of personal spiritual experience and experiential piety for all Christians. Many have understood the spiritual experience of "conversion" or "rebirth" (regeneration) to be essential. American Protestants, especially in more popular expressions such as revivals and in contemporary television evangelism, but also in more routine church life, have particularly emphasized this "affective" or emotional aspect of religious life. Some have made spiritual experience their central emphasis. Quakers seek the quiet inner light. Holiness churches strive for the experience of moral sanctification (purity) in the spiritual "second blessing." Pentecostal churches find the manifestations of the spirit in the "speaking of tongues" and in faith healings. Though some also seek spiritual experience through sacramental practice—as is central in Roman Catholicism, such as the Eucharist (communion, or the Lord's Supper)—for most Protestant traditions the Bible is the primary nurturing resource for personal spiritual experience and piety in the life of the church. Preaching, praying, singing, and community interaction are the ways to affect people's spiritual awareness and condition; and Protestants are busy doing all of these things.

Fourth, we can locate a characteristically Protestant understanding of the church. With great variations, the Protestant traditions have thought of the church not so much as a sacred and authoritative institution as a *gathered* congregation of believers freely associating for public worship, mutual ministry, growth in spiritual-intellectual-moral life, and for corporate mission in the world. Regardless of how institutionally complex and bureaucratically organized aspects of Protestantism may be, the church essentially is defined as all of the people consciously associating voluntarily in the name and experience of Jesus Christ.

Fifth, in its development—first within European Christendom, from there to nations of the world, and westward across the North American continent—Protestantism has thrived as an aggressive mission movement. As Protestants have encountered the world's other religions, as they have competed among themselves and with others for church members and support, and as they have responded to conditions of human needs and suffering, they have engaged in what they understood to be expressions of Christian mission. As we will see fully displayed in California history, Protestant energy for evangelism (proclaiming the Gospel), proselytism (making converts), propagation (spreading their influence), and benevolence (charitable works) has assumed innovative forms and methods.

Of course these characteristics by which we are trying to identify California Protestantism are found also in all traditions of world Christianity everywhere throughout history. They also are not all clearly or equally expressed in any particular Protestant group. But they are historic emphases that Protestants have expressed persistently in various ways, priorities over which they have competed, cooperated, divided, and united. They reflect the Reformation "ethos" that has permeated Protestant life and thought. They help us recognize Protestant Californians when we see them, as distinct from Roman Catholics or Eastern Orthodox Christians.

As we observe the life of California Protestants we will detect marks of their independence and individuality, of their emphasis on activities of the laity in the total life of the church both gathered and dispersed in society, and of their preoccupation with the Bible and spiritual experience. We will recognize their corporate worship by how they try to involve all of the people in biblical reading, preaching, singing, and praying. This worship experience will happen in church sanctuaries, in homes, or almost anywhere, with or without an ordained minister or priest, always with the anticipation that a person's mind and emotion will be spiritually moved. We also will see Protestants, along with other Christians, involved in many sorts of ministry and mission activities, through church-related institutions and independent of them, responding to human needs both directly and through influencing the institutions and structures of society.

Unfolding California Protestant Life

California Protestantism made its first energetic appearance in the San Francisco Bay area as "the world rushed in" after the discovery of gold. San Francisco became an "instant city," transformed from a frontier outpost to an urban center during the 1850s and 1860s, surrounded by boom towns in all directions. Within the struggle for social order and cultural formation, Protestant voices and institutions joined with many others.

Denominational Plantings

Methodists, Presbyterians, Congregationalists, Baptists, and Episcopalians were earliest on the scene, followed soon by Unitarians, Lutherans, Quakers and Disciples of Christ. Most of these were descendents of earlier British and northern European settlers east of the Rocky Mountains in the United States—the vanguard of the westward-moving Republic. But some were new immigrants from Germany and Scandinavian countries, for example, making their new American home in California. Among the newcomers, too, were black Afro-American pioneers and Chinese immigrants, who broadened the ethnic spectrum of Protestant communities.

So the pattern was set at the start. A cosmopolitan, pluralistic social environment would challenge Protestants' ingenuity for vital community organization. The Bay Area thus became the first regional center of most denominations in the state. As the Bay Area continued to grow and expand its influence throughout the Far West during the later nineteenth century, these early Protestant plantings spread and produced off-shoots in all directions.

Meanwhile, the transcontinental railroad (completed in 1869) altered the California Protestant social landscape measurably in the years following. The Los Angeles area experienced the first of its population explosions that have continued to the present day. With people came churches, and all of the northern-planted denominations took root in the south as well. By sheer numbers, Los Angeles has been the center of California Protestantism since the early twentieth century. As we shall see later, however, the Protestant experience has differed in the two regions, as has so much else of California culture. In addition to this broad regional difference, pockets of distinctive Protestant life also have developed in particular locations throughout the state from San Diego to Santa Barbara, Fresno to Modesto, Bakersfield to Stockton, Redding to Eureka.

By the early twentieth century, holiness and pentecostal churches such as the Church of the Nazarene and the Assemblies of God had become new California denominations. By then, too, well established communities of Mennonites and the Church of the Brethren could be found in various scattered locations; while the "new immigration" of southern Europeans and Japanese again broadened the spectrum of Protestant ethnic plurality.

Then as people again swarmed into California (now also by automobile) during the 1920s and 1930s, the Protestant population became increasingly complex. The Great Depression added misery to the victims of dust-bowl droughts in the southern mid-West, and many migrated to California. Then followed the lure of West Coast shipyards and other industries during World War II, again adding to the state's population. Among the newcomers, white Southern Baptists and African Americans bearing black church traditions made a major new impact on California Protestant life. Since World War II the California population again has exploded, not only with a continuous westward movement but also with those moving eastward across the Pacific from Southeast Asia and northward from Central America. They too have enlarged the panorama of California Protestant life.

Institutions, Associations, Movements

Denominational traditions only partly express the range of California Protestants' life. There seems to be no limit to their ingenuity in organizing for special purposes and objectives. Essentially, however, these organizations fall into two categories: denominational and church-related (ecclesiastical) institutions, and non-ecclesiastical associations. To complicate matters further, Protestants frequently have used the word "movement" to refer to more-or-less organized activities and commitments that cut through and also bypass denominational, church, and other institutional structures that otherwise identify their loyalties.

Protestantism is first and foremost a church-centered religion. Its ongoing life germinates primarily from local congregations. There people find stability, continuity, and flexibility that correspond to the order, rhythm, and disruptions of their common life. There, too, traditions actually live; they are preserved, challenged, and reformed. Congregations provide opportunity for all kinds of people to practice their faith in a corporate context, to participate in community life, to express a functioning religious identity in their larger social lives.

Beyond local congregations there are denominational affiliations, though the independent (or denominationally unattached) local community church is not uncommon in California. Most denominations are organized on local, state, regional and national levels, and some maintain international ties. In this way members of local congregations find larger contacts through interlocking religious networks that, for example, engage otherwise provincial Californian Protestantism with national and global expressions of its life. As the denominations have found ways to facilitate relations with one another through interdenominational federations and councils, moreover, California Protestantism has further expanded into realms of ecumenical (worldwide Christian unity) and interfaith cooperation and dialogue.

Finally, churches and denominations extend organized Protestant life into a myriad of related institutions for activities and purposes otherwise beyond the reach of local congregations. Within weeks after the first Protestants arrived in California, for example, they were making plans to establish schools, hospitals, and specialized missions. Today the state is dotted with these and many other kinds of church-related institutions through which Protestant life and thought reach into the larger realms of California society.

But Protestantism is not bound to ecclesiastical structures. Through voluntarily supported associations and societies without reference to churches' power and authority, Protestants organize and act to fulfill particular commitments and goals. These include social, economic, political, cultural, as well as specifically spiritual interests. Thus we find Protestants involved in most aspects of California life and thought, private and public, on most sides of most issues, as groups and coalitions, and as individuals. Protestants have found still other ways to sort themselves out into identity groupings that to the world-at-large sometimes may seem to be their major public visibility. These "movements" nearly become traditions in their own right with both ecclesiastical and non-ecclesiastical associations. Fundamentalism, for example, is not only a set of doctrines and an interpretation of the Bible as literal, inerrant truth; it also is a popular movement capable of garnering a social-political-economic agenda. Not all television evangelists, faith healers, prophets of doom or success are particularly Protestant; but many project identities that both polarize Protestants and create coalitions of Protestants, within and outside of the churches.

People

In the final analysis, we do well to search for the Protestant tradition in California by locating its variety of adherents—its people. An apparent truism sometimes is forgotten by those who define and analyze religion. A religious tradition does not exist in the abstract, but only as it is believed and practiced by particular people living in particular times and places. The denominations, churches, associations, and movements thus are best known by the people involved in them.

Protestant Californians, the people themselves, are even more difficult to generalize about than is Protestantism as a religious tradition. A few individuals who reached national and even international fame as religious personalities in California history personify the variety of Protestant identity. In their own minds as well as in the minds of others, such persons as Thomas Starr King, John Muir, Aimee Semple McPherson, and Bishop James A. Pike pressed the borders of Protestantism in several different directions. (Their stories will appear in the chapters that follow.) Like so many others, they came to California from other places, here to discover new religious frontiers. The many lesser known but no less significant leaders of churches and "movements," plus the countless faithful (and not-so-faithful) members and supporters of those religious institutions and commitments, make up the historic lifeblood of California Protestantism.

Because they are human beings—men and women, children and adolescents, all races, ethnic groups, and socio-economic classes—Protestant Californians have lived their faith imperfectly. Their motives, perspectives, passions, and biases have been as mixed as have any peoples,' so that their professed beliefs and ideals often seem muddied in the historical records of their actual lives. But on the whole Protestants have known this fact about themselves. When their professed doctrines of sin and of God's forgiving grace in Jesus Christ have become their spiritual faith experience, so as to inspire them to strive for a higher quality moral-ethical life, then they have embodied Protestant Christianity as an historic, living religion.

Protestants Among Other Californians

Having identified and located Protestantism as an historic religion in California, it remains for us to gain a perspective of Protestants among the totality of Californians. Statistics of religious groups are notoriously imprecise, but they do support several facts that will help us understand the historical nuances of California Protestant life and thought (1980 statistics).

First, approximately 35.7 percent of California citizens are affiliated with churches or synagogues—far below the national average of just under 50 percent. Second, just under 36 percent of these religiously affiliated Californians are Protestants, compared to over 58 percent who are Roman Catholics. Protestants, therefore, comprise the major minority of California Christians. Third, though Protestants number far fewer than do Roman Catholics, they are much more numerous than any other religious group in California. Mormons are about 5 percent of religiously affiliated Californians, Jews about 0.7 percent, and all others together well under 1 percent.

The "all others" category, however, while small in numbers, is a fourth significant factor in the California religious environment. Since the mid-nineteenth-century beginning of statehood, California has experienced a wide plurality of such religious groups. Islam, Buddhism, Hinduism, and dozens of new religious movements both imported and indigenous to the United States (some born in California itself) flourish alongside the Jewish and Christian traditions. Many of these groups became very visible in recent decades, but the fact is that California has long been attractive to religious groups lying off the mainstream.

By any count, therefore, Protestants are but a minority of California's total population—about 12.5 percent, or just under 3 million. No doubt many Californians who consider themselves to be religious while maintaining no religious affiliation (perhaps another 15 percent of the population, according to surveys) would embrace a more or less Protestant identity. Nevertheless, Protestants by any definition are relatively few in number among Californians as a whole. However, we shall see in the chapters that follow that they are highly visible, energetic participants in California's cultural history.

PROTESTANT PROPORTIONS OF CALIFORNIA POPULATION

	California Population	Protestant Communicants	Protestant Percentage
1890	1,213,398	92,953	8 percent
1906	2,034,859	193,178	9 percent
1916	2,938,654	305,363	10 percent
1980	23,688,049	2,200,000	9 percent

SUGGESTED FURTHER READING:

Ahlstrom, Sydney E., ed. *Theology in America: The Major Protestant Voices from Puritanism to Neo-Orthodoxy.* Indianapolis and New York: The Bobbs-Merril Company, Inc., 1967.

Bainton, Roland H. *The Protestant Reformation In The Sixteenth Century.* Boston: The Beacon Press, 1952.

Brown, Robert McAfee. *The Spirit of Protestantism.* New York: Oxford University Press, 1961.

Chadwick, Owen. *The Reformation.* New York: Penguin Books, 1972.

Dillenberger, John and Welch, Claude. *Protestant Christianity.* New York: Macmillan, 1988.

Ernst, Eldon G. "Religion In California," *Pacific Theological Review* XIX (Winter 1986).

Hatch, Nathan O. and Noll, Mark A., eds. *The Bible in America.* New York: Oxford University Press, 1982.

Hopewell, James F. *Congregation: Stories and Structures.* Philadelphia: Fortress Press, 1987.

Hudson, Winthrop S. *American Protestantism.* Chicago: The University of Chicago Press, 1961.

Hughs, Richard T. *Illusions of Innocence: Protestant Primitivism in America, 1630-1875.* Chicago: The University of Chicago Press, 1988.

Marty, Martin. *Protestantism.* Garden City, N.Y.: Doubleday, Image Books, 1974.

Richey, Russell E., ed. *Denominationalism.* Nashville, Tenn.: Abingdon Press, 1977.

Spitz, Lewis W. *The Protestant Reformation 1517-1559.* New York: Harper & Row, Publishers, 1985.

2 California Protestants in World Context

On March 1, 1931 a marble statue of Thomas Starr King, popularly known as California's "apostle of liberty," was unveiled. The state legislature had named King and Junípero Serra to be California's two permanent representatives in the Hall of Statuary at the nation's Capitol in Washington, D.C.

What an appropriate choice of persons so to honor, for together they symbolized the watershed in California history that came with statehood in 1850—a turning point that also marked the formative time of California Protestantism. If Serra (1713-1784), the energetic Franciscan founder of Catholic missions on the Spanish-Mexican frontier, represented Old California, then King (1824-1864), the liberal Unitarian Protestant preacher-orator, social humanitarian evangelist, and patriotic advocate of the Union cause in the Civil War, represented the new U.S. American California. The mission legacy of the old would give way to the new as California looked toward the twentieth century.

This 1931 declaration of California heroes also was timely. It called attention to California's strategic location within the modern course of world events, including the shifting geographical patterns of Christianity. Over eighty years of statehood had seen California flourish into a major socio-economic-political center in the nation with its own international connections. The Protestant churches had participated in these developments through their institutional networks that channeled the visionary ambitions of their people. Yet by 1931 the world had plunged into a state of social-economic-political crisis with far-reaching effects on religious movements and organizations of all kinds. The world, it seemed, was in upheaval, and California was feeling the impact.

A hint of this upheaval could be found in the mid-nineteenth-century transition from old to new California, symbolized in the brief but dramatic career of Thomas Starr King. In 1860, on the eve of the nation's War Between the States centered on the issue of slavery, King resigned his Hollis Street Unitarian Church pulpit in Boston to move 3,000 miles across the continent to the Unitarian Church in San Francisco. Immediately his preaching and oratorical skills captured the imagination and spirit of a large public within and outside of the church. With North and South hotly represented among California's pioneer settlers, the state's Civil War posture was uncertain (on July 4, 1861, for example, the Confederate flag flew over the Los Angeles Plaza). Speaking persuasively up and down the state, King helped rally Californians to the Union cause. His subsequent labors for social humanitarian causes, including his support of the oppressed black and Chinese San Francisco minorities, brought him due credit for engendering a measure of moral "civilizing" influence in the burgeoning young society. When exhaustion led to pneumonia and his early death in 1864, the state legislature adjourned for three days in mourning, and some 20,000 people came to pay tribute as he lay in state. Though remembered for patriotic service, however, King's historic significance as a pioneer Protestant church leader lies also in his benevolent ministry that embraced the new California interaction of Anglo-Europeans with Africans, Asians, and Hispanic people.

Moreover, that cultural interaction would take global expression as well. From California's Pacific shores, church missions would reach out to distant lands with increasing vigor as the twentieth century dawned, reaching a height of international momentum before being disrupted by World War I. Thereafter, California Protestants would find themselves engaged in new kinds of relationships with Christians in, and from, other lands.

The California Protestant experience must be portrayed within the dynamic framework of modern Christian world mission history. But to understand something of the world outlook and sense of identity that many Protestants brought to their California experience, we again must recall their heritage, beginning especially with the migrations of Old World European Christians to the New World of the Americas.

European Christendom Transplanted in America

Well over 200 years before Protestants began to settle in California, certain of their ancestors had made their way across the Atlantic Ocean from Old England to a New England wilderness. Those early "pilgrims" were part of an unfolding saga, as throughout the seventeenth and eighteenth centuries North America became a stage for the colonization of European peoples. Christendom having been divided by Protestant Reformation and Catholic Counter-Reformation, they came with distinct national-religious identities.

Christendom, by simple historical definition, was that part of the world in which Christianity was the prevailing religion. European Christendom defined much of western civilization for centuries. The church, in its rich varieties, permeated most aspects of culture and was assumed to be the central unifying force in society. When European Christendom exploded in the sixteenth-century Reformation, just as the age of European global explorations began, Protestants and Roman Catholics assumed competing and conflicting roles of defining and extending Christian society.

Because the very notion of Christendom implied both a Christian citizenry and a Christian social order, the agents of its expansion combined religious and civil institutions. Together (in harmony and in conflict) sword and chalice, soldier and missionary, magistrate and cleric led what they thought to be the advancement of Christian civilization. The medieval holy crusade and spiritual pilgrimage joined in the modern extension of Christendom from the Old World to the New World. Catholic New Spain and New France especially competed with Protestant New England for control of Colonial North America—for the formation of an American Christendom.

New England, New France and New Spain

The majority of those who settled in the Atlantic seaboard colonies that eventually became the United States were British and (to a lesser extent) northern European Protestants; and most of them were influenced by the Calvinist Reformed tradition, though some were Lutherans. Predominant in New England were the British nonconformist Protestants—Congregationalist Puritans, Presbyterians, Baptists, and Quakers who had dissented from the established Church of England (Episcopal) seeking a more radical reformation than the Anglican tradition expressed. A variety of Dutch, Scandinavian, and German Protestants of Reformed, Lutheran, and radical sectarian traditions settled in the middle colonies along with the British denominations and a relatively small number of English Roman Catholics.

From the earliest years Anglicans were established in parts of the South, and eventually they developed strong parishes throughout the colonies. During the later eighteenth century Presbyterian and Baptist churches began to prosper from missions in the South, and following the American Revolution the Methodist movement of spiritual revival and moral discipline within Anglicanism (inspired by John Wesley) had been organized into a new independent denomination. Soon Methodists were everywhere in the new nation and on the westward-moving frontier.

In addition to the relatively few English Catholics and even fewer Jewish settlers, two racial minorities added diversity to the populace. Native American Indians were being pressed into circumscribed frontier areas, some having been converted by Christian missions but most remaining outside of (and oppressed by) the dominant Anglo-American society. Most Africans, having been brought to the Americas as slaves throughout the colonial period, remained in bondage in the South, though a small number were free. Through missions and associations with white culture, a minority of blacks both slave and free had become Christians. By the end of the eighteenth century a few free black Methodist and Baptist congregations had formed in northern cities, as well as spiritual associations among southern slave communities that mixed African with European-rooted cultures into an indigenous American expression of Protestant Christianity.

The churches of Colonial America along the Atlantic seaboard, however, were predominantly Anglo-Protestant. Together they would so permeate the early nineteenth-century westward-moving American culture as to become known as the Protestant mainstream—a cultural-religious identity that in more recent years assumed the label "WASP" (white Anglo-Saxon Protestant). While a clear majority east of the Mississippi River, therefore, on the far western California frontier Protestants of this powerful cultural-religious heritage would become especially conscious of their own ethnic-religious identity; here they came into intimate contact with peoples of southern European, Mexican, Asian and Pacific Island, and African heritages. Included in this multicultural mix were Protestant, Roman Catholic, Russian Orthodox, Mormon, Jewish, and Buddhist religious identities.

Anglo Protestants never had been the only bearers of European Christendom in North America. For two centuries preceding the American Revolution, Spanish and French Catholic empires had surrounded the British Protestant colonies. This contest for control of North America had exaggerated the Protestant versus Roman Catholic attitudes among Christians.

In the East, French-British relationships predominated. By the late eighteenth century the French Catholic empire in North America had declined to near extinction through a series of wars, treaties, and retreats. Thereafter the colonial French heritage was confined to Quebec in the north, though leaving cultural remnants in New Orleans at the southern part of the Louisiana Territory. But that territory extended as a vast triangle from the mouth of the Mississippi River in the south, northward into the Great Lakes region, then westward to the Columbia River in the Pacific Northwest, with French Catholic marks along the way.

In 1803 the United States purchased the Louisiana Territory from France, and three years later the Lewis and Clark expedition explored the region to its Pacific coast shore. This was the first United States overland contact with the Far West, just north of California in the Oregon territory, where soon both French Catholic and Anglo-Protestant missions would be planted. Though trails opened between Oregon and California by the late 1830s, little traffic passed over them until the mid-century gold rush. Though French ships had probed the California Coast, no settlements resulted. There the impact of French Christianity, both Protestant and Catholic, would be felt only with new European immigrations following statehood. Colonial New France thus made no direct impact on California Protestantism.

But New Spain was another story. Hispanic Roman Catholicism had planted itself firmly in much of Central and South America since Spanish *conquistadores* and missionaries began arriving in the early sixteenth century. Throughout the eighteenth century missionaries and military explorers pressed northward from Mexico into Texas and the southwestern territories of present-day United States. About the time of the American Revolution they began establishing missions, *pueblos* (towns), and *presidios* (military outposts) in California. Inspired by Junípero Serra, between 1769 and 1824 a total of twenty-one Franciscan Catholic missions were planted in California soil from San Diego in the south to Sonoma in the north. After Mexican independence from Spain in 1821 the missions began to decline—a process that continued through the Treaty of Guadalupe Hidalgo (1848) that ended the United States' war with Mexico and brought California into United States possession by annexation. Still, the Hispanic Catholic culture lived on among the *Californios* as California became a state in 1850, after which it became overwhelmed and displaced by the flood of immigrants of different religious-ethnic backgrounds.

It was during this period of transition from Hispanic Mexican to Anglo-American frontier during the 1840s and 1850s that Protestants began to settle in California. Here was a *frontera* heritage of social systems, economic structures, and religious piety foreign to their previous experience. Here was a meeting of two conflicting bearers of European Christendom in North America.

The American Protestant Christendom Impulse

From the perspective of California Protestants, this historic Christendom competition took a momentous mid-nineteenth-century turn when the Hispanic Mexican *frontera* became the Anglo-American frontier. They came to California imbued with visions of forging a Christian America that had motivated Anglo-Protestants since the Puritans first landed in New England. Those early American Protestants consistently had articulated their sense of participating in the unfolding of a new Christian civilization. They had understood their "errand into the wilderness" to be the fullest and purest expression of reformed Christianity in a new world frontier—a "city upon a hill," a "light to the nations" for the world to observe and emulate.

The Puritans' interpretation of their new world role became deeply ingrained in Colonial American Protestant consciousness. It was a visionary and aggressive Christendom that readily became transferred to the new nation, as in the famous 1783 election-day sermon entitled "The United States Elevated to Glory and Honor" preached by Yale College President Ezra Stiles, who prophesied that the American Republic would "illuminate the world with truth and liberty, as part of God's providential conversion of the world." But it was Connecticut preacher Thomas Brockway who in 1784 most vividly set the Protestant Christendom vision in a larger, though still limited, historical and geographical perspective:

> Empire, learning and religion have in past ages been travelling from East to West, and this continent is their last Western stage; the great Pacific ocean which bounds the Western part of the continent, will bound their further progress in this direction. Here God is erecting a stage on which to exhibit the great things of His Kingdom, the stage is spacious, the territory extensive, such as no other part of the globe can equal. . . . When we consider above three thousand miles of western territory, the most fertile part of America, yet uninhabited, can we not suppose this is the wilderness and the solitary place that shall be glad and the desert that shall bloom as the rose. [*America Saved, Or Divine Glory Displayed In The Late War With Great Britain* (1784), p. 24.]

The land, of course, was not uninhabited but home to many native tribal peoples; and the westward movement would not stop at the Pacific Coast. But Brockway's vision was compelling.

Looking westward across 3,000 miles of wilderness, descendants of those colonial American Protestants adopted this national religious consciousness for their own. They came to share a sense of embodying and building an American Christian civilization as they joined the westward movement. They planted new churches and stretched their denominational networks. They built colleges and seminaries (to train clergy). They formed societies for benevolent and social reform goals. They organized and promoted various evangelistic programs, disseminating literature, holding public worship in railroad chapel cars, staging mass revival meetings to reach the unchurched and revitalize the churches. And as the nation itself expanded westward, annexing new territories under the ideology of "manifest destiny," it became common for Protestants to intertwine their religious and civil identity. Theirs, they thought, was a Christian civilization in-the-making.

So it was that nineteenth-century Protestant pioneers prepared to enter the California frontier. They thought of themselves as pilgrims of the Pacific in a new age. All of the symbols and images of the British-Spanish Christendom contest came to focus on California. The most benevolent Protestant interpretation described California as "a child of Spain" and Father Serra as the "California Knight of the Cross," preparing the way for Christian progress in the expanding American Republic. The more harsh, triumphalist view was that Spanish Catholicism represented vestiges of Old World medieval darkness, now to be replaced by the purified New World Anglo-Saxon Protestant Christian light. These Protestant pilgrim-pioneers thus brought a vision of a new California to be molded into "the beacon of the world" by cross-bearers of the Reformation spirit.

When they spoke of "the vast importance to the whole world of the annexation of California to the United States," moreover, they assumed that establishing a strong Protestant church life in the new California was vital to what they perceived to be the nation's manifest destiny in the expansion of Christian civilization throughout the world. The key to this Protestant vision was *mission*—California's place in the modern world Christian mission enterprise.

The Protestant World Christian Mission

When Protestantism made its first permanent entry into California at mid-nineteenth century, it hardly could be called a world religion. The vast majority of Protestants still lived in western Europe and the eastern third of North America. Yet by then these provincial boundaries were in the process of bursting open. Protestant movement into California was part of a vast explosive international mission movement that would alter the religious map of the world. Some historians even speak of the "great century" of Protestant world mission expansion, meaning roughly the nineteenth century, or more precisely 1815-1914. (Parenthetically, as the twenty-first century approaches, religious geographers note that neither Europe nor North America but Africa and South America are the centers of world Christian growth and vitality, with spectacular Christian stirrings also occuring in parts of Asia.)

The Great Century

This modern Protestant world expansion began during the late eighteenth century in the context of British imperial claims in India. Soon British missions took hold also in Australia, New

Zealand, and Pacific Islands. As the nineteenth century progressed, British missionaries entered South Africa, China, and eventually Japan, Korea, and the Philippines. Continental European nations (such as Denmark, Germany, France, and Holland) also sent missionaries. But the British missionaries, such as the legendary William Carey in India and David Livingston in South Africa, were most widely known among American Protestants.

Meanwhile, the American churches themselves also became involved in overseas missions. As clipper ships returned to Boston and other Atlantic seaports from trade voyages in the Pacific, missionary fervor swept early nineteenth-century Protestants. In 1812 a party of young New Englanders, supported by the newly founded American Board of Commissioners for Foreign Missions, sailed for India. Among them were the newly married Adoniram and Ann Hasseltine Judson, who were converted to Baptist views during the voyage, and whose subsequent mission to Burma stimulated the American Baptist denomination to organize a foreign mission society to support them and other Baptist missionaries. By mid-nineteenth century most denominations were sending and supporting missionaries overseas as part of their normal ongoing life.

These were the agents of Protestant "foreign missions." They were called "foreign" because they went to lands outside of Christendom, places where Protestant Christianity was a foreign religion and where Christians of any kind were at most a small minority of the population. As Europeans once had looked to the Americas as a foreign mission field, so now American Christians looked to South Africa and Asia as their foreign mission fields. As the American denominations formed "home mission" boards and societies to facilitate their westward expansion across the North American Continent, so they also formed "foreign mission" boards and societies to facilitate bringing their expression of the Christian gospel to the people (evangelizing non-Christians) on other continents and to organize indigenous churches.

The Protestant foreign missionary movement emanating from Britain, Europe, and North America increased at an accelerating rate during the later nineteenth- and early twentieth-century period, reaching a height of intensity and popular momentum just on the eve of World War I. As the British and European churches rode the crest of their nations' influence in other parts of the world, the North Americans extended their Christian "manifest destiny" ambitions concretely through feverish mission activity accompanying the United States' rise to international power. The Spanish-American War (1898-99), for example, brought the United States into a dominating position in the Philippines, where American Protestant missions gained a permanent foothold. But the key to understanding the globalization of Protestantism that took place during that half-century lies in the churches' interlocking cooperative mission organizations on an interdenominational and international basis. Their goal was to "evangelize the world," a missionary motive that fueled what became known as the Ecumenical Movement (striving for world Christian unity).

In each of the "home base" nations the organizational patterns took similar development. Denominations formed mission organizations (boards, societies, etc.). These joined into cooperative councils or federations, such as the German Evangelical Mission, the Conference of Missionary Societies of Great Britain and Ireland, and the Foreign Mission Conference of North America. At the same time, mission movements specifically among women and among college-aged young people fostered similar organizations. (Missions became a powerful context for the flourishing women's movement of the day.) The Christian vocational idealism and energy of young adults became channeled through such organizations as the Young Men's and the Young Women's Christian Associations, and the Student Christian Federations. In the United States, as in Europe and Britain, recruitment and support for the missionary enterprise was garnered as well through non-denominational "movements," such as the Student Volunteer Movement for Foreign Missions (from college campuses), the Missionary Education Movement, and the Laymen's Missionary Movement.

The larger dimensions of this world Protestant mission thrust found structured interconnections in the international expressions of these various agencies: The World's Alliance of the YMCA, the World's YWCA, and the World's Student Christian Federation, for example. Even more far-reaching were the international missionary conferences that began as early as the 1850s. British, European, and American missionary leaders came together seeking ways to cooperate on "the field," to pool their knowledge and experience in order to avoid competition in or duplication of their missionary efforts. The New York City conference in 1900 brought nearly

200,000 people together for ten days from over 200 mission societies. Even more significant was the 1910 World Missionary Conference in Edinburgh, because for the first time it included official delegates from mission societies plus representatives from churches outside of Britain, Europe, and North America—the so-called "Younger Churches" of Asian and African nations. Out of this conference was born the International Missionary Council to carry on the joint international enterprise and to meet periodically in various parts of the world. A veritable international Protestant missionary army thus had been amassed for what they understood to be their role in the expansion of Christianity throughout the nations of the world.

Twentieth-Century Upheavals

The First World War (1914-1918) marked a transition in Protestant world missions. The British and European churches' role in the movement began to decline, while the North American churches assumed a leading role. (In 1910 North Americans comprised one-third of all Protestant overseas missionaries, or about 7,200; in 1925 the percentage rose to over one half, or 15,000 of 29,000 total.) Moreover, international Protestant gatherings increasingly expanded beyond churches of the western nations. When in 1928 the International Missionary Council met in Jerusalem, one-fourth of the delegates were from the "younger churches." Ten years later (1938) the "younger churches" contributed one-half of the delegates, and the conference was held in India. Also, foreign missionaries from American, European, and British churches became increasingly a minority among mission leaders in Asian and African countries. These lands outside of Christendom thus were becoming transformed from foreign to home mission fields.

This shifting pattern of international Protestantism has become even more striking since World War II, given the momentous changes in the postwar world. Revolutions in India and China have led to national political independence, and likewise the peoples of Africa and South America began asserting their independence. With these international upheavals has come a shift in the cutting edges and centers of growth in world Christianity, including Protestantism. The indigenous, independent churches of Africa now make up perhaps 7 percent of the total world Christian population, and Protestantism there is being profoundly affected by this phenomenon. In Latin America, Protestant Pentecostalism is growing rapidly alongside (and in increasing contact with) new indigenous expressions of Roman Catholicism. Some are calling this movement a "new reformation" generating a "theology of liberation." The churches of such Asian countries as China, India, and Korea likewise are making an impact on world Christianity. European-rooted traditions are being reborn and renovated by being translated, transformed, and integrated into cultures outside of Western Christendom; and now by migrants and immigrants these are being brought to California—yet another mixing of new with old Protestant traditions.

Since the 1948 formation of the World Council of Churches, the gatherings of this ecumenical movement increasingly have expressed the diffusion of Protestant Christianity throughout the world. Churches of the "third world" nations (the "younger churches") have shared aggressively in the Council's agenda, and nationals from these countries have assumed greater control of their own churches. Where American overseas missionaries have continued to increase (nearly 40,000 career persons in 1985), such networks as the "Third World Missions Advance" (organized in 1988) are taking greater initiative. The mission, therefore, no longer is simply directed from the Western Churches to those of Third World countries. Rather, Christian interaction moves in all directions; and world Protestantism thus reflects the socio-political revolutions of the twentieth-century world.

We can conclude that, in one sense at least, the Protestant foreign mission enterprise succeeded: the world was evangelized. In ways not fully envisaged by nineteenth-century western missionaries, indigenous churches emerged in nations outside of Christendom. By mid-twentieth century Protestantism was well along the way to becoming a truly world Christian religion—an historic process reflected in the evolving California Protestant experience.

California Expressions of World Protestantism

From Friday evening through Tuesday noon, July 25–29, 1975, several hundred California Protestants gathered for the sixty-second annual Pacific Southwest Conference on World Christian Mission at the Asilomar Conference Grounds in Pacific Grove, located on the beautiful central California coast near Monterey and Carmel (site of a Franciscan mission). The conference integrated themes of the upcoming "American Bicentennial and the Church: A Celebration in Tension," with "Southeast Asia: A Christian Presence." The two keynote theme speakers came from Berkeley and Burma, respectively. Already the 1976 United States Bicentennial year conference themes had been announced, centering on "People and Systems: China, Cuba, Tanzania and the U.S.A." The annual interdenominational conferences at Asilomar thus rehearsed and stimulated the California Protestant mission heritage, maintaining connecting links between its home and foreign dimensions.

California Protestantism was born of mission passion, was nourished by mission imperative, and became permanently marked by mission enterprise. At least three factors help account for this mission orientation: (1) the timeliness of California's Protestant origins and early development; (2) California's geographical location; (3) the continual migration of people of many nationalities and ethnic identities to California.

The Time, the Place, the People

Within the context of "the great century" of world Christian expansion, California Protestantism was born in the "fullness of time." The first phase of missions to Africa and Asia had passed, and this meeting of East and West had planted seeds of "younger churches." Likewise the growing new American nation had made its initial westward thrust, reaching the Pacific through successive conquests and annexations of Texas-New Mexico, Oregon, and California territories. Only a young nation, enamored of its resources and opportunities, could interpret all of this with the audacious vision of "manifest destiny." In this spirit California's pioneer-pilgrim Protestants identified with the global implications they had seen in their "timely" entrée into the land of new-found gold. They marveled at their fortunate opportunity of being in "a prominent and peculiar position for evangelizing the world." They had heard the call issued in 1849 from New York, for example, by the *Baptist Home Mission Record*:

> Go where the waves are breaking
> on California's shore
> Christ's precious gospel taking,
> more rich than golden ore

To those who came and thought religiously about their adventure, California became "the beacon of the world" as "a field for missionary effort unsurpassed by any other in the world."

Not only the time, but also the combination of place and people indelibly stamped the California Protestant mission sensibility. Geographically California's Pacific location—"the sea of the future"—struck nineteenth-century church leaders as the most strategic point of departure for overseas missionaries. That the traffic moved in both directions further enhanced the mission opportunity. A distinctive characteristic of the new California from its beginning was the incoming population's range of national and ethnic diversity, which struck early California Protestants as a potent mission field—"a great missionary nursery," in the words of Congregationalist pioneer Joseph Augustine Benton. Here the foreign and home fields overlapped: "The home field has extended westward, and the foreign field eastward," they noted, "till they seem almost to touch."

Missions to Chinese, both in China and in California, especially commanded the early Protestants' attention. Many Chinese immigrants, like others who rushed to California for gold and for economic opportunity-in-general in later years, had thoughts of returning home. Many did leave, but many more stayed. In either case, they presented a mission challenge to the Anglo churches, as described by the *Pacific Banner* in 1852: "Great numbers from every foreign people are coming among us. . . . They need such influences here as shall speedily enlighten and convert them to Christianity. . . . Thus converted and enlightened, they will be qualified to return to their countrymen and labor for their conversion." As for the Chinese in particular, seventy-five years later (1927) a California Presbyterian educator, Edward Arthur Wicher, reflected on the continuing mission to "the Orient in California."

> The work on behalf of the Chinese in California has consequences far beyond the limits of our state and nation. Particularly does the coast of China feel the result. Many make a periodical visit to their kinsfolk in China and be it said to their credit, they always take their religion with them. And scores of Christian preachers in China have been converts in the mission of America." [*The Presbyterian Church In California 1849-1927* (1927), p. 315]

The fact that lively Buddhist temples had been established along the California coast only added urgency to his mission advocacy.

Over the years this sense of evangelizing the world in and through California became extended to include other Asian and Pacific Island peoples, as well as southern and eastern Europeans, Mexicans and other Hispanics, and "foreigners" from wherever. Indeed, the very concept of "foreigners" became obscured as California newcomers persistently comprised the major portion of the overall population, both within and outside of the churches. From the mid-nineteenth century to the present day it has not been uncommon for California Protestants to describe their "foreign mission field at home" as being as much outside of Christendom as within it. Always a minority, but with an inherited Christendom vision, Protestantism in California has partly reflected its world expansion beyond Christendom.

The Mission Enterprise

In order not to overstate the mission aura of California Protestantism, some qualifications are in order. The visionary rhetoric of church leaders always inspired relatively few to an equally enthusiastic response. From pioneer days to the present many Protestant Californians have shared the "laid-back" attitude of their regional culture, and nominal church members have often remained unconcerned about "missions." Indeed, stimulating their own people to committed churchmanship, including zealous evangelism, has been consistently a part of the spoken mission imperative of countless Protestant leaders. The perceived secular environment, plus the plurality of religious cultures foreign to Anglo-Protestant traditions, have added to this mission field mentality. Mission thus has been an organizing principle and impetus in California Protestant thought and history, even though the cultural climate and population dynamics have worked against the odds of making California "Protestant."

Later chapters will describe more of the range of Protestant mission activities. Here it is important to recognize the Protestant response to California itself as a kind of world mission field—a response that helped produce indigenous expressions of ethnic minority churches among immigrants to California from around the world.

To summarize, Protestant denominations first established themselves in California as missions. The first regional organization was the Methodist Annual Mission Conference, organized in 1848, a year before evangelist William Taylor began his work in San Francisco. Protestant Episcopal Bishop William Ingraham Kip came in 1854 to a Missionary Episcopate. Meanwhile Congregationalist Joseph Augustine Benton, Baptist Osgood C. Wheeler, Presbyterian Samuel Hopkins Willey, Lutheran Jacob Buehler, and African Methodist Episcopal John J. Moore were among the better-known pioneer church builders—all missionaries by job description. Eastern-based denominational mission boards—often foreign boards at first—supported much of the work. As frontier communities became transformed into cosmopolitan societies, local church congregations and parishes functioned as mission outposts, and regional denominational structures helped establish specialized mission programs at home and overseas.

Presbyterians illustrate the general Protestant pattern of relating home and foreign mission activity on both sides of the Pacific in their work with Chinese people. The work began with Chinese leadership—persons converted to Christianity in China by American missionaries. Lam Chuen, arriving in San Francisco in 1851, stimulated the Presbyterians to action by his labors among the immigrant community. In 1853 a Presbyterian church in Chinatown was organized by William Speer, an appointee of the Presbyterian Board of Foreign Missions. The denomination brought seasoned foreign missionaries, such as Ira M. Condit, from China to work in California. In 1883 the California Branch of the Women's Foreign Mission Society (founded in 1873) sent Mindora Berry, a native Californian, to China. Donaldina Cameron then became famous for her work with Chinese girls in San Francisco, beginning in 1895. Meanwhile, within fifty years the Mission Society had sent over 135 Presbyterian women overseas. The denominations' work with Chinese set the pattern for similar missions among Japanese immigrants by the 1880s and among Korean immigrants beginning in 1905. Foundations thus were laid for the building of Asian American Protestant churches in twentieth-century California.

By the turn of the century, too, Southern California Protestants had become involved in mission work with Hispanic people. In 1897 the interdenominational California Spanish Missionary Society was organized, with Alden B. Case of Pomona its first "general missionary." His published pamphlet described the mission as "Foreign Work at Home for Our Spanish Neighbor." The Presbyterians, Methodists, Baptists, Disciples of Christ, Congregationalists, and the Pentecostal Churches joined in the Hispanic mission enterprise.

California Protestants celebrated their combined "home" and "foreign" world mission role at the 1915 Panama Pacific American Exhibition. Drawing on the past and forecasting the future, the exhibition displayed how the Hispanic-Anglo Pan American cultural interaction had assumed new dimensions, reaching out across the Pacific to Asia and Pacific Islands as well. San Francisco, freshly rebuilt from the 1906 ruins of earthquake and fire, conceived and promoted the international event; and interdenominational California Protestantism, through its Committee of One Hundred, contributed to the exhibition's religious dynamics. Religious congresses on women's missions and on immigration specifically reflected Protestant mission concerns, while religious and anthropological exhibits mirrored more general Protestant identification with national progress and cultural mission to the world. Overall, progressive optimism carried the day, but this was about to be sorely tested.

By 1915 the world had gone to war on European battlefields. Two years later the United States entered the conflict "over there," and American Protestants joined the patriotic victory campaign to "make the world safe for democracy" (as President Wilson phrased it) and, they hoped, safe also for the final spread of Christianity among the nations. Such was the world vision of the American Christian mission enterprise in 1915, with California at its frontier edge.

But time would reveal the more complex course of national and world events then taking place. The decline of Europe's global expansion and domination had begun, and the United States' rise to world power seemed imminent, though not uncontested. Immediately after the war, the newly-formed Interchurch World Movement of North America united thirty American Protestant denominations to raise money and personnel to complete the world mission process that the war had disrupted. California Protestants joined this post-war campaign. Their 1919 Asilomar world missionary conference, sponsored partly by the Interchurch World Movement, presented militantly triumphalist themes of "Christian

Americanization," "world Christianization," and "nothing less than the complete evangelization of all of life."

It might be said then that American Protestant optimism thus survived the Great War, but only momentarily, for it soon was dashed by disintegrating conditions both at home and overseas. The Interchurch World Movement went bankrupt and failed by the end of 1920. Soon it was clear that a new era had dawned for Protestants in America as well as in Europe and throughout the world. While the United States entered a period of isolationism in its international relations (never joining the League of Nations, for example), Protestant missions continued, but with less certainty (and plenty of debate) about their goals and methods, and with emerging new results on the horizon.

By 1930, moreover, the United States had fallen from the "roaring twenties" prosperity to a great economic depression of international proportions, and the churches suffered along with social institutions generally. Already California had received thousands of nearly destitute migrants from the southern Midwest, with no new "apostle of liberty" having emerged among the struggling churches. In 1931, therefore, when the State Legislature was to name its two representatives for the Hall of Statuary, it looked to the past for heroes.

Economic relief would come, first with the Federal "New Deal" programs of the Roosevelt Administration, but finally only at the great cost of a second world war. After the bombing of Pearl Harbor in 1941, the United States entered the war, to be fought in Pacific and Atlantic battlegrounds in both northern and southern hemispheres. Again California's social fabric received major alteration as wartime industries drew many thousands into the State.

Prominent among the newcomers were large numbers of African American citizens migrating westward seeking wartime employment. They greatly bolstered the size and numbers of black churches in metropolitan areas, bringing a fresh resurgence of distinctively Afro-American religion into California Protestant life—mostly Baptists, Methodists, and Pentecostalists.

Post-World War II society then presented major new challenges to California's churches, as did the changed international scene. Throughout the twentieth century California's domestic-international connections have expanded. Emigrants from Japan, India, Korea, the Philippines and other Pacific Islands, and most recently from Southeast Asia and Central America have extended both the California Protestant mission agenda and the spectrum of ethnic churches. The overall picture ties California Protestantism to the world mission expansion of the past two centuries.

As in China, India, South Africa, and other regions outside of Western Christendom, California has produced its own ethnic plurality of "younger churches" alongside the older British-European-rooted traditions. Hispanic and Chinese Baptists, African and Japanese Methodists, Korean Presbyterians, and many other ethnic minority Protestant denominational churches have thrived in California. Most were born of Protestant missions both overseas and in California. To varying degrees most have remained part of the parent denominational networks, conscious of their minority status, while developing interdenominational ethnic associations as well. In 1950, for example, the Japanese Evangelical Missionary Society was formed to evangelize Japanese people in the United States, Japan, South America, and worldwide. During the 1970s, Asian American caucuses were organized in several denominations. At the same time an interdenominational Pacific and Asian Center for Theology and Strategies was organized in Berkeley to relate to issues in the Asian American communities and to help train Asian American Christian leaders.

Tragically, Anglo-Protestants, like white Americans generally, often had related to those whom they perceived to be "foreigners" in prejudiced and discriminatory ways, though mission leaders usually defended minorities from disabilities within the civil order. It is not surprising that during the past quarter century Asian, African, and Hispanic Californians have declared their Christian liberation from control by Anglo church power structures. Their resurgent cultural-religious identities must be understood in the context of the coming-of-age of "younger churches" in Third World countries, including their commitment to independence and to movements of social-political-economic and spiritual liberation.

California Protestantism, therefore, may be more authentically pluralistic today than ever before. As such the pattern of its mission-orientation by necessity has been changing. Since the 1960s most denominations have dropped the "foreign mission" label in favor of such names as "international missions" or "global ministries." The idea of equal partners in world mission that has been challenging ecumenical Protestantism both within and outside of

Western Christendom applies also to California Protestants. Mutual ministry among diverse churches, perhaps an extension of the doctrine of the "priesthood of all believers," may become the guiding principle of organized California Protestantism in world context.

On March 1, 1889 the Reverend O.C. Wheeler, one of California's earliest pioneer missionaries, looked back forty years in describing those pioneers to the California Baptist Historical Society. Noting that "slow and toilsome and disappointing as [had been] the progress of our mission in California," still the achievements were encouraging when set in historical and geographical context.

> The Mayflower landed her Pilgrims on Plymouth Rock, 200 years before these pioneers entered the Golden Gate, and the results of that event have ever since been celebrated as a marvel of modern civilization. But, excepting the promulgation of certain religious tenets, they can no more be compared with the work of these California pioneers, in celebrity of action, in breadth and scope of achievement, in the great march of human progress, than the State of Massachusetts can geographically compare with California. No more than the old mail stage coach can compare with today's telegram. [*The Story of Early Baptist Beginnings in California* (1889), p. 8]

In Wheeler's thwarted yet dogged optimism regarding those pioneer-pilgrims' time and place in human history, we can detect something of the distinctive flavor of California Protestants' sense of identity that continues to the present—to which topic we now turn our attention.

SUGGESTED FURTHER READING:

Anderson, Gerald H. "American Protestants in Pursuit of Missions: 1886-1986," *International Bulletin of Missionary Research* 12 (1988).

Beaver, R. Pierce. *American Protestant Women in World Mission: History of the First Feminist Movement in North America.* Grand Rapids, Mich.: William B. Eerdmans, 1980.

Carpenter, Joel A. and Wilbert, R. Shenk, eds. *Earthen Vessels: American Evangelicals and Foreign Missions, 1880-1980.* Grand Rapids, Mich.: William B. Eerdmans, 1990.

Crompton, Arnold. *Apostle of Liberty: Starr King in California.* Boston: Beacon Press, 1950.

Handy, Robert T. *A Christian America: Protestant Hopes and Historical Realities.* New York: Oxford University Press, 1984.

Hogg, William Richey. *Ecumenical Foundations: A History of the International Missionary Council and Its Nineteenth Century Background.* New York: Harper and Brothers, 1952.

Hutchison, William R. *Errand to the World: American Protestant Thought and Foreign Missions.* Chicago: The University of Chicago Press, 1987.

Latourette, Kenneth Scott. *A History of the Expansion of Christianity,* vol. 4, *The Great Century in Europe and the United States of America A.D. 1800-1914.* New York: Harper and Brothers, 1941.

Lavender, David. *California: Land of New Beginnings.* Lincoln, Nebraska: University of Nebraska Press, 1972.

Loofbourow, Leon L. *In Search of God's Gold: A Story of Continued Christian Pioneering in California.* San Francisco and Stockton: College of the Pacific, 1950.

Marty, Martin E. *Righteous Empire: The Protestant Experience in America.* New York: The Dial Press, 1970.

May, Henry R. "The Religion of the Republic," chapter 9 in *Ideas, Faiths, and Feelings: Essays on American Intellectual and Religious History 1952-1982.* New York: Oxford University Press, 1983.

Niebuhr, H. Richard. *The Kingdom of God in America.* Chicago: Willett, Clark & Company, 1937.

3 The Impact of California on the Formation of Protestant Identity

"**Go** where you may within the bounds of California," wrote naturalist John Muir in *The Mountains of California* (1894). "Mountains are ever in sight, charming and glorifying every landscape." He then tried to characterize his beloved Sierra Nevada Mountains in the midst of California's alluring geography:

> Making your way through the mazes of the Coast Range to the summit of many of the inner peaks or passes opposite San Francisco, in the clear springtime, the grandest and most telling of all California landscapes is spread before you. At your feet lies the great Central Valley glowing golden in the sunshine, one smooth, flowery, lake-like bed of fertile soil. Along its eastern margin rises the mighty Sierra, miles in height, reposing like a smooth, cumulus cloud in the sunny sky, and so gloriously colored, and so luminous, it seems to be not clothed with light, but wholly composed of it, like the wall of some celestial city.

Muir (1838-1914) symbolizes some important aspects of California as a place of Protestant identity. Like the majority of Californians since the 1840s, he migrated to the state. Born in Scotland, his family moved to Wisconsin when he was eleven, and after extended journeys on foot throughout the land as an adult, he reached California in 1868. Although he lived in California the rest of his life, he continued to roam the wilderness areas of the Pacific

Coast from the Mexican border north to Alaska. His restlessness only underscores the persistent mobility of Californians.

Neither a church-goer in California nor a subscriber to a conventional creed, Muir did not abandon the austere Presbyterian religion he had inherited. His perspectives, lifestyle, and vocabulary were infused by patterns derived from the Bible. Though consciously unorthodox, they resembled the romantic naturalism and intuition of his eastern American contemporary, Ralph Waldo Emerson. A writer and preacher of nature, and the preservation of nature, his sense of mission reflected California Protestant characteristics. In 1892 he founded the Sierra Club, which became something of a quasi-church where true believers gathered to learn, to meditate together in club outings, and to support the mission to conserve natural resources through publications and political lobbying.

Muir's nature theism thus bordered the fringes of California Protestantism, yet his religiosity suggests that Protestantism in California, perhaps more than in most places, had extended beyond adherence to formal religious institutions. It also highlights California as a geographical and social landscape that has played a role in reshaping Protestant religious identity.

The California Landscape

The Physical Landscape

The English word "landscape" derives from a Dutch word, *landschap*, which literally means the condition of the land. California's physical landscape is remarkable for its variation. Third in overall area to the states of Alaska and Texas, California encompasses the extremes of Mt. Whitney (14,495 ft. above sea level) and Death Valley (282 ft. below sea level), of over 100 inches of rainfall annually in the northwest corner of the state and 2 inches in the southeast corner. The 1,264 miles of coast, significantly broken only by the confluence of waters that form the Delta and the San Francisco Bay, are lined with mountains, timbered in the north and matted with brush in the south. Muir's "Range of Light"—the Sierra Nevada—runs along the eastern edge of much of the state. It absorbs the moisture from Pacific storms and in turn waters the fertile Central Valley that lies between it and the coastal ranges. At the southern end of the great interior ellipse are mountains lying generally east-west. Inland and to the south of these is a vast arid region of mountains, valleys, and plains.

The geographical subregions of California, with their varied vistas, flora, and fauna, are impressive, as is the overall climate. Little rain falls between April and November, and only in the high mountains are winters harsh. Summers in the interior are hot, but along the coast, fog, sea breezes, and relatively low humidity make for mild year-round temperatures. Most of California experiences a climatic year effectively dominated by two instead of four seasons: a mild rainy season and a mild-to-hot dry season.

To varied scenery and a generally temperate climate is added an abundance of natural resources. Agriculture has largely dominated the California economy since Spanish settlement in the eighteenth century. The rich soil of the Central Valley, the Salinas Valley, and the Imperial Valley in particular have come to sustain, with the help of widespread irrigation after 1890, a staggering diversity of livestock and crops: cattle, sheep, cotton, hay, and a plethora of fruits and vegetables. Lumbering and fishing also have been important economic activities in the state. The climate itself has proved to be an economic resource. Good weather has been pivotal, for example, in the origins and growth of tourism, movie production, and the aerospace industry in California. Finally, extractive industries have been significant. In the twentieth century, dominance in this area has gone to oil recovery and refining. From 1848 to 1870 gold mining reigned supreme, though ironically the only lasting fortunes from that period were derived not from gold but from commerce, railroads, and agriculture.

The Social and Cultural Landscape

The 1848 discovery of gold in California's physical landscape caused a decisive alteration of the region's social and cultural landscape. It immediately led to the peopling and exploitation of the Sierra foothills, the settlement of parts of the Central Valley, and the "instant" urbanization of the northern end of the San Francisco peninsula. Partly because of its rapid growth, California did not pass through the territorial stage before being admitted as a state in 1850. A new California society, generally dominated by modern urban-oriented social structures and cultural perspectives, swiftly buried the prior agrarian society of Spanish-Mexican California, which already had marginalized the earlier hunter-gatherer societies of Native tribes. U.S. American California superimposed on the physical landscape a social and cultural landscape that, in the words of historian Kevin Starr, was irrevocably linked "imaginatively with the most compelling of myths, the pursuit of happiness."

American-born migrants and foreign-born immigrants alike have inundated California since 1848 in pursuit of happiness. San Francisco was California's largest and most dominant city until the third decade of the twentieth century. It also has been a major entry port for immigrants. One out of every three San Franciscans in 1870 had been born in Ireland, Germany, China, or Italy, and between 1870 and 1930 over half of the city's population had foreign-born parents. More recently, the revision in 1965 of U.S. immigration laws has contributed to making the metropolitan area of San Francisco by the mid-1980s the nation's locale with the greatest proportion of new immigrants. San Francisco has thus exerted remarkable social and cultural influence in California not just during the latter half of the nineteenth century but also the first decades of the twentieth. Out of a total state population of 865,694 in 1880, for example, nearly two-thirds of Californians lived north of the Tehachapis, of which 233,959 resided in San Francisco, while only 11,183 lived in Los Angeles. Twenty years later, the situation had changed only slightly, with only some 325,000 out of 1,485,000 Californians living in the South.

By 1920, however, Los Angeles and Southern California had caught up with and surpassed San Francisco and Northern California in population. Aided by the completion of the railroad connections to the East, Los Angeles and Southern California attracted ever increasing numbers of migrants. Los Angeles' population quadrupled in the 1880s to 50,000, then doubled in the 1890s, tripled in the 1900s, and doubled in the 1910s and 1920s. During the 1920s, 1.3 million people moved to Los Angeles, most arriving by automobile, a phenomenon described by historian Gunther Barth as "one of the great internal migrations in the history of the American people." By 1930, the City of Los Angeles had some 1,238,000 people, some 2,319,000 in its metropolitan region, compared to San Francisco's 634,000 in the city proper and 1,290,000 in the metropolitan area. Particularly between 1890 and 1920, thousands of prosperous families from the rural Midwest—states such as Indiana, Illinois, Iowa, Nebraska, and Oklahoma—responded to the intense advertising of Southern California land promoters and moved to the region in search of health, self-fulfillment, and in many cases a modestly leisured retirement. They flocked to California sunshine from the places of cold winters and blistering summers. As the Gold Rush had given the San Francisco region an enduring cosmopolitan tone, a place for tourists and settlers alike, so the midwestern migration to Los Angeles gave that city and its metropolitan region a persistent flavor of comfortable conservatism that was open to innovation in the pursuit of the good life.

U.S. American California life, of course, has always been rural as well as urban. There developed rural-oriented towns in the coastal and inland farming regions and in the sparsely settled far north and mountain areas. Often people bound together by religious and ethnic culture, especially those of smaller, distinctive, or newer denominations, sought out agricultural districts relatively isolated from urban centers.

Danish Lutherans, for example, at the turn of the century founded Ferndale in the far north and Solvang in the south, both near the coast. Seventh-Day Adventists, organized in 1863 to emphasize sabbath observance on the seventh day (Saturday) plus dietary and other health restrictions, clustered around St. Helena, Healdsburg, and Angwin in the Napa and Russian River valleys. Whittier was colonized in the 1880s by members of the Society of Friends, or Quakers, with seventeenth-century British roots emphasizing the spirit's "inner light" in each person, silent corporate worship, and a pacifist ethic. Settlements of German Baptist Brethren (or Dunkers), stemming from a radical pietist movement seeking to recover New Testament-ordered church life, clustered around Lordsburg, later renamed La Verne. Mennonites, founded in the sixteenth-century Netherlands as a radical disciplined Christian community withdrawn from the rest of the world, settled in the Central Valley around Reedley after the turn of the century. Some Presbyterians tried to found a "God-fearing community" of farms in Southern California, naming the settlement Westminster after their denomination's seventeenth-century English Puritan catechisms and confessions. (Westminster now is adjacent to the Los Angeles International Airport.)

Such isolated rural communities seeking to preserve distinctive religious integrity have been a constant California phenomenon to the present day. Historically, rural and small town life tended to sustain traditional ways, because social change and cultural diversity were slowed in their effects on rural areas. Important factors in this slowing include geographical distance from the urban centers of change and by the reinforcement of tradition which came through the daily patterns of a local community. People experienced a bonding network of social relations providing a shared understanding and sense of obligation. The same people worked, played, learned, and worshipped in churches together.

This kind of small-town social experience has not disappeared in California, and very distinctive communities continue to exist. Yet isolation has proved hard to maintain. The social and cultural dominance of urban centers in the state has increased with population growth, illustrated by the fact that Whittier, La Verne, and Westminster, for example, have been absorbed into greater metropolitan Los Angeles. A 1945 San Francisco Bay Area church study noted the increasing modification of rural culture by "urban incursion into the country." Modern mass media—printed magazines and newspapers, radio, and television—has broken down the possibility of isolation. Rapid transportation, especially freeways for auto travel, has allowed people employed in cities to live in ever more distant towns. Moreover, modern life has become increasingly segmented. For example, economic success through following a modern occupation often means leaving one's original locality and moving from place to place in a career track. The occupation itself is not controlled locally, and work relationships are not communal in nature. Occupational life puts a premium on efficiency, adaptability, and performance. Work life is separated from other aspects of life. People who work together do not normally see each other in school, at the store, in their leisure time, on their home street, or in church. Their overall life experience is expanded by the variety of people they meet in various aspects of their lives, and by the public mass media. As will be seen, all of these aspects of modern life, so prominent in California's history, have deeply affected the nature of Protestant church life.

Also important in California's social landscape have been the historical patterns of migration and immigration to and within the state. Since Gold Rush days and the later midwestern migrations to Southern California, the inrush of new people has been a constant California experience. The experience has been rural as well as urban. A 1922 study of religion in the two agricultural counties of

Orange and Stanislaus noted that their populations were drawn from all over the world. "Occident and Orient meet here. Nearly every state in the union is represented." Large-scale agriculture has drawn in various groups to harvest the crops: first the Chinese, until they were legally excluded in 1882; then the Japanese, who were partially restricted in 1907; for a brief time East Indians; then, since 1917, Mexicans. "Okies" fleeing the devastating dust bowl storms and droughts in the southern Great Plains migrated to California in the 1930s.

World War II brought thousands of military personnel and workers to urban areas for shipbuilding, aerospace, and other war-related industries. From this migration California's population of African American citizens increased by 300 percent in five years. Then followed the nuclear and high tech industrial booms, drawing great numbers of highly-skilled workers to California urban areas during the post-world war decades. In 1962 California surpassed New York as the most populous state, with no sign of decreasing growth. During the 1970s and 1980s, following the Vietnam War and the modifying of immigration restrictions, massive immigration of Southeast Asian people and Central Americans has again greatly altered the California social landscape.

Meanwhile, California became one of the nation's early twentieth-century cultural pacesetters. The Hollywood-based entertainment industry disseminated and reinforced the advance of a lifestyle of self-fulfillment through consumption. Southern California's "car culture" accentuated individual mobility and helped create the dispersed, suburban sprawl of greater Los Angeles. Planned cities, motels, shopping centers, and drive-in movies, banks, diners, and churches took decisive shape in California and spread across the country.

In the 1960s, some of the teenaged "baby-boomers" (those born during the late 1940s-early 1960s) in Southern California created a "beach culture," while others in the North gave direction to the new rock music (the Grateful Dead, etc.), to the "hippie" counterculture (the Haight-Ashbury, following San Francisco's "Beat" movement of the 1950s), to "new consciousness" of human potential (like the Esalen Institute), and to radical social protest—the Berkeley Free Speech Movement, People's Park, the Black Panthers, the Symbionese Liberation Army. In the 1970s and 1980s, the California electronics industry, centered in the "Silicon Valley" of the Bay Area, helped reshape both work and leisure in the U.S. with computer and other technologies.

California continues to be a place of growth and change. The San Francisco Bay Area has replaced Philadelphia since 1980 as the fourth largest metropolitan area in the U.S., while Los Angeles is the second largest. In Los Angeles the majority of the population soon will be of non-European ancestry. In this remarkable, ever-changing social environment in which modernization consistently has challenged all traditionalism, California Protestant identity has taken shape.

California's Formative Impact on Protestant Identity

Protestants and the Physical Landscape

Like John Muir, Protestants responded to the California landscape, which contributed to the formation of their distinctive religious identity. When the great migrations to California began in the 1850s, romantic perspectives were deeply influential in Anglo American culture. Romanticism appreciated nature and wilderness as necessary counterbalances to civilization. Increasing numbers of people became enamored with nature as wilderness—whether as an ideal, or as a regular vacation from the city, or, in the case of a few such as John Muir, as a way of life. Protestants in California discovered an especially rich context in which to develop such views.

Unitarian Thomas Starr King (introduced in chapter 2), a religious liberal of his day, emphasized God's immanence or presence in nature instead of the more traditional stress on God's separateness from nature and human life. (Liberalism is discussed in chapter 4.) California's rich agricultural resources impressed him, but the grandeur of the Sierras overwhelmed him. Nature, in his view, was an expression of divine mind, and the Yosemite Valley was a revelation of divine beauty and moral heights. "So many of us there are," said the popular preacher in the 1860s, "who have no majestic landscapes for the heart—no grandeurs in the inner life. We live on the flats. . . . We have no consciousness of Divine, All-enfolding Love. We may make an outward visit to the Sierras, but there are no Yosemites in the soul."

King's use of the Yosemite as a moral metaphor and spiritual analogy soon became a Protestant convention, particularly among the more liberally inclined. By 1916, Herbert Atchinson Jump, pastor of Oakland's prestigious First Congregational Church, merely restated Thomas Starr King when he urged everyone to make life "a miniature Yosemite by surrounding each day's experience with high places." Presbyterian editor Arthur Pierce Vaughan was typical of more Orthodox Protestant views. For him, nature as seen in a Yosemite camping trip was wholesomely recreational rather than divinely revelatory. "Age, if you will, with nerve strain in the cities," he editorialized in 1911, "but come and grow young loafing here with Nature." But it was John Muir who most captured the Protestant religious sense of California's natural beauty.

Muir's religiously-infused descriptions of Yosemite, for example, were sources for Protestant exaltation. In extolling a Yosemite vacation, Vaughan, the conservative, could not resist quoting at length Muir's description of the valley's falls as "white banners, shouting, rejoicing, arousing every rock and crystal of the mighty walls to throb and tingle in glad accord."

Jump, the liberal, gave a nod to Muir for what Jump understood as the "exquisite insight" of Yosemite as a natural temple. As early as 1879, the California Sunday School Association collected funds to erect a Yosemite Chapel, so that Protestantism could maintain a formal presence in Muir's wilderness church.

More significantly, Muir's conservationist gospel had notable Protestant supporters. Joseph LeConte (1823-1911), nationally known as a natural scientist and a proponent of the compatibility of theism and evolutionary theory, was a close friend of Muir and a leader of the Sierra Club. LeConte had come to join the new University of California faculty in 1869. Escaping his native South after the devastation of the Civil War, LeConte found California a "wonderful new country, so different from any that [he] had previously seen, the climate, the splendid scenery, the active energetic people, and the magnificent field for scientific, and especially for geologic investigations." LeConte had been raised in a strict southern Presbyterian home, but like Muir, as an adult he turned away from confessional orthodoxy. Unlike Muir, however, he spoke for a more liberal faith from within the church. A charter member of Berkeley's First Presbyterian Church, he and his family maintained active membership there until his death, which came while he was on a Sierra Club trip to Yosemite in 1901.

Another Protestant associate of Muir's was William F. Bade

(1871-1936). Raised a Moravian Protestant, in 1902 Bade assumed the post of professor of Old Testament at the Congregationalist Pacific Theological Seminary in Berkeley. A well-known biblical scholar and archaeologist, he also edited the *Sierra Club Bulletin* from 1910-1922, served as president of the club from 1919-1922, and was Muir's literary executor, publishing *The Life and Letters of John Muir* in 1923-1924. With a mystical spirituality, he saw Muir as a "prophet and interpreter of nature and nature's God."

Not only its landscape but California's climate also attracted Protestants' attention. David Starr Jordan (1851-1931), a Unitarian who so admired Thomas Starr King that he took "Starr" as his middle name, came to California in 1891 as the founding president of Stanford University. A popular speaker and writer in addition to his administrative and teaching duties, Jordan blended a moralistic but undogmatic Protestantism with an optimism about the potential of scientific expertise in fostering a biologically vigorous people. In an 1898 article in the *Atlantic Monthly* magazine, he told a national audience that "the charm of California has, in the main, three sources—scenery, climate, and freedom of life." Extolling his adopted state, he claimed, "As there is from end to end of California scarcely one commonplace mile, so from one end of the year to the other there is hardly a tedious day." With less exaggeration, he added, "the climate is especially kind to childhood and old age."

Most Protestant migrants to Southern California after 1880 would have agreed with Jordan. Janetter Lewis Young, for example, moved to Los Angeles with her Presbyterian clergyman husband in December of 1884. "When we reached Los Angeles and saw the bright sunshine all day long," she wrote in her diary, "and the trees and flowers as fresh as in summer, we could not realize Christmas is near." In declining health—she died the following year—Young confessed, "How grateful I am for the warmth and light of the sun. It is already taking the chillness out of me and making me feel stronger."

Climate and not just social-economic opportunity has regularly been behind much of the attractiveness of California. The Presbyterian missionary for Southern California in the late 1880s-early 1890s recalled that "It was easy to find a minister for every field." He had to warn off ministers who inquired, telling them, "Don't come to California unless you have to for your health, and then simply come and take your chances when here."

Some California Protestants actively promoted the region's healthfulness. Best known was Ellen G. White (1827-1915), the prophetess of the health-oriented Seventh-Day Adventist Church, who fell in love with Northern California in 1872 and retired to St. Helena in 1900, giving her approval of the state as a healthy place. George Wharton James, Long Beach Methodist pastor during the 1880s, later wrote books setting forth a gospel of outdoor living and organic diet that he based on his understanding of the ways of the Native Americans of the Southwest and his perceptions of what most fitted the Southern California environment.

In general, then, Protestants responded positively to the allure of the California natural scene. The Christian belief in God as creator of all that is good, together with the dominant idealistic and optimistic mentality of Americans in the late nineteenth and early twentieth centuries, made it easy for many Protestant Californians to understand the land and climate as expressive of God's bountiful glory and love. Representative of this perspective is a poem entitled "Primeval Redwoods" by Carrie Judd Montgomery, who came to the Bay Area in 1890. Already a leader in the faith healing movement within conservative Protestantism when she arrived, after the turn of the century she became a regional leader of the new pentecostal movement (chapter 4). She loved to spend time on land that she and her husband owned among the redwoods north of the Russian River at Cazadero. She wrote of the giant trees ("Primeval Redwoods"):

> Ye oracles of God! Full well ye preach your weighty sermons, eloquent and wise; In strong, unuttered words, in forceful speech. Your thrilling presence masters all my soul.

Montgomery interpreted the redwoods in moral terms consistent with her conservative religious views:

> Your slow, sure growth of centuries shows forth that holy patience that inspires the soul when fully taught of God. Your upright trend, and straight, undeviating forms shame all who fail to show integrity of life.

California redwoods were subsumed into Montgomery's views of the divine direction of history toward judgment and recreation of all of life by Christ:

> With mission new in God's restored, new earth, ye still shall rear

your heads, and join the song which morning stars voiced on Creation's Day, and which shall burst afresh in wondrous joy, to Him who comes and claims His right to reign. [*Heart Melody* (1922), pp. 41-42]

In a more liberal theological vein, Presbyterian minister John E. Stuchell wrote in a 1910 *Pacific Presbyterian* article that "if Jesus had no other claim to reverence" than his "wondrous love of nature, it would be incumbent upon California to adopt him as its patron Deity, and to rear temples in His honor." Stuchell then articulated what perhaps many other California Protestants have sensed: "This is an outdoor country, and if religion is to dominate it, it must be an outdoor religion."

Yet even the most optimistic Protestants have felt some peril and temptation in the midst of California's environmental blessings. Congregationalist John Wright Buckham, theology professor at the Pacific School of Religion for many years, undoubtedly spoke for many Protestants when in 1907 he praised California's "generous soil . . . genial air . . . fair sky . . . noble mountains . . . and vast ocean [that] stretches before us its pathway to larger intercourse and opportunity." However, Buckham also made a characteristically Protestant warning in the midst of his paean to California: "All this, without idealism, and honor, and consecration, means temptation, corruption, coarse and conspicuous failure. With faith, with devotion, with God, it means something very like the true Utopia."

Buckham's warning reflected a concern of many Protestant leaders about the ease with which people could feel comfortably at home in the California environment without involvement in the church. "Life seems prosperous without religion," wrote a Presbyterian minister in 1893, "and there is a tacit conviction cherished by many that religion is not so important but that one can get along very well without it in California." In tension with their outspoken praise of the natural environment was the frustration many Protestant leaders felt in trying to foster church attendance on Sundays. A notice in the October 7, 1917 bulletin of Bethany Congregational Church, San Francisco, illustrates how the land and climate worked against traditional church attendance:

Sunday some people were observed leaving for an outing. One observer was heard to remark with surprise, "They attend Bethany

Congregational Church and are leaving before service." The "world" has little conscience on the Sunday exodus question, but even there the feeling exists that Christians ought to come to church first. When a Christian finds himself below the world's standard it's time to think—probably to halt.

Protestants could not help but be aware of the physical allure of California. In their general agreement with non-Protestant neighbors in finding the environment attractive, Protestants did not merely conform to secular sensibilities. The Protestant cosmology (view of the order of reality) enabled their acceptance of the landscape and climate as gifts of a good Creator. Enjoyment of California's environment heightened many Protestants' optimism about divine purposes for the world and this life. Yet their inherited understandings of sin and temptation also kept alive in them an undercurrent of dissatisfaction with California's pull of people away from traditional church practice and belief. The problem for church leaders was "to make the people love the Lord as they [did] the climate." These tensions in their life and thought have appeared even more sharply with reference to California's social and cultural landscape.

Protestants and the Social and Cultural Landscape

The experience of rapid, humanly-defined urbanization surrounded by awesome, divinely-created natural environment presented California Protestants with a certain dilemma. At home in nature, how could they be equally at home in the secular city? Deeply ingrained in their inherited sense of identity was their mission-like aspiration to Christianize their American social environment. Yet it was this aspiration, along with their sense of "at home-ness" in the dominant culture of the eastern regions of the nation, that was most challenged by the social and cultural landscape of California.

For some Protestants, not being fully at home in California society was nothing new to their American experience. African Americans, for example, remained as much outsiders in California as they had always been "strangers in their own land" before and after the Civil War. Though few in number until World War II migrations, black Californians had struggled for their basic civil rights and equality from mid-nineteenth century on, with Protestants in the thick of it. In 1915 the pastor of the North Oakland Baptist Church, Gordon C. Coleman, wrote in the Oakland *Tribune* that "of all places that [blacks] should not be discouraged is here in California, a place favored of God." Yet they were discouraged, Coleman noted, because "the disposition in these parts is to give [black people] an opportunity to spend a dollar but refuses to permit [them] to make one."

Black Protestants, in other words, like other racial minorities, wished to participate in California's promise of a better life, but prejudice and discrimination undercut their attempts. The Anglo majority among Protestants only gradually came to realize the presence of other Protestants in California's social and cultural landscape. When Anglo Protestants spoke of their aspirations for a Christian society in California, therefore, their vision was less than inclusive of even all Protestant legacies.

Anglo Protestants, nevertheless, were bold in articulating their religious and social aspirations for California. Addressing the New England Society in San Francisco in 1852, Presbyterian minister Timothy Dwight Hunt invoked the Puritan tradition as a guide for Protestant identity and activity. "Sons and Daughters of New England," spoke Hunt, "you are the representatives of a land which is a model for every other. . . . No higher ambition could urge us to noble deeds than, on the basis of the colony of Plymouth, to make California the Massachusetts of the Pacific." A half century later (1906) Claiborne M. Hill, president of the new Pacific Coast Baptist Theological Seminary in Berkeley, appealed to the Protestant missionary impulse to motivate his Baptist audiences toward goals similar to Hunt's:

On Thanksgiving day I climbed the hills back of Berkeley. . . . I saw a cluster of cities populous and prosperous. I saw a great harbor, its fair bosom flecked with the white sails of pleasure yacht and fishing craft, its wharves lined with the great ships and ocean liners, and its gate-way opening wide to the commerce of the world. Heavy trains thundered along the tracks of the shore line, speaking convincingly of the state and continental resources lying northward and southward and eastward. At my feet lay the academic town and the great University. . . . I saw the world through the eye of the harbor . . . yonder islands of the sea, the nearer ones the scene of missionary achievement . . . the farther group over which our flag but yesterday began to wave . . . the rising millions of China groping for the light of which Christian America is able to give. . . . And I said to myself, if I could have our Baptist hosts here upon this hillside for an hour . . . they would get a new sense of the present and coming greatness of the Pacific Coast; they would come to a new sense of the meaning of the Christian's mission on these shores of the setting sun; they would feel more keenly than ever before the need of trained leaders for our churches; and for our neighbors across the ever narrowing Pacific. [*Arise and Build* (1943), pp. 47-49]

Hill, however, spoke more out of traditional Anglo Protestant hopes than out of California cultural-religious realities. Protestant aspirations for a Christian California always confronted the state's religious pluralism and public secularity; statistics betrayed the social weakness of their attempts to shape California society. The U.S. Religious Census of 1916 summarized church membership figures, which totaled about 30 percent of the state's population. Only about one-third of these, or 10 percent of the state's population, were Protestant church members. These figures, moreover, would remain about the same in the decades ahead. California never has been a predominantly church-related or church-attending society, and Protestant churches have never represented more than a minority within the minority of church-affiliated Californians.

California Protestants, therefore, never constituted a large enough percentage of the state's population to make their aspiration for a "Christian California" plausible. Protestant strength did succeed in dominating turn-of-the-century Los Angeles for awhile, but increasing secularity during the 1920s, plus diverse and ceaseless immigration to the region since that time, have eliminated any possibility of an Anglo-Protestant cultural establishment. Instead, the state's traditional dominance by its cosmopolitan and religiously pluralistic urban centers since 1849 made for a social landscape in which Anglo-Protestants never felt like the dominant religious mainstream that long reigned over much of the eastern and midwestern United States. This sense of being relative "outsiders" clashed with their inherited self-identity as religious "insiders."

Not that Protestants were oppressed or treated with hostility. Rather, church leaders complained of being ignored, tolerated along with other religious and secular groups, but treated with widescale indifference. They were torn between lamenting the fail-

ure of California to conform to their Protestant vision of a righteous society on the one hand, and their sense of California's
promise for the good life on the other hand. "What are we to
become?" asked a Presbyterian editorialist in the *Occident* in 1888,
"a Christian people, or a people of Baal?"

California, it seemed, could go either way. After the turn of the
century, the Methodist editor of the *California Christian Advocate*
could intone a litany of failings against San Francisco in 1909:
"There is no city in the Union more heavily handicapped by dominant religious forces [non-Protestant, meaning Roman Catholi-
cism], low moral ideals, bad leadership, commercial incoherency,
political demoralization, social incompatibilities, class antago-
nisms, bitter race hatred, Sunday desecrations, a towering defiant
whiskey oligarchy, a wide, superficial, frivolous, vaudeville spirit,
than San Francisco." But then Baptist Robert Whitaker at the same
time could extol California's possibilities: "Half of the irreligious-
ness of California is itself religious. Idealism springs naturally in
this lovely land of ours. . . . The weakling may perish here if his
imported religion is a mere veneer. But the Abrahamic soul may
still find its Canaan in the West, beside the waters of the world's
last Mediterranean, the 'Great Sea' of the morrow, and the 'chosen
people' of God had never nobler conquest before them, nor
promise of larger reward than here." Whitaker's article, appearing
in *Sunset Magazine* in 1906, amid the earthquake ruins of San Francisco, spilled over with hope for the future:

> But the spirit of a happy and holy inspiration broods over the land,
> and the world of tomorrow shall not only get its commerce by way
> of the Golden Gate, but forth from our city of Saint Francis, and
> our city of the Angels, there shall go the songs and prophecies of
> the world's best faith, and the evangel of a blessed hope and a glo-
> rious destiny for the race.

In 1916 there appeared a remarkable large volume entitled *The
Lutheran Church And California*, edited by E.M. Stensrud, pastor of
Trinity Evangelical Lutheran Church in San Francisco. The book
presents a short history of Lutheran churches in California, with
reference to their mid-western and eastern denominational centers,
and introduces outstanding Lutheran personalities in California's
religious and secular life. The book then launches into an encyclo-

pedic description and analysis of California's marvelous climates, geography, and natural resources ("Mother Nature left little for man to accomplish") plus chapters on agricultural, horticultural, business and educational opportunities. The book's purpose is to inform migrating people, especially those of Lutheran identity, of California's opportunities for building new homes, communities, livelihoods, and churches. It notes that many migrating Lutherans had gone astray: Families coming to California often are "swallowed up . . . in this maelstrom of materialism and—in all matters spiritual—indifferentism, so prevalent and dominating in these regions of the Western Coast." The argument intends to stimulate California Lutheranism, to bring wayward California Lutherans back into the churches and to encourage Lutherans from other places to migrate to California. The book ends like an elaborate travel brochure, describing scenic routes to California by rail and by ship. California was thus presented to Lutheran Protestants as an unprecedented combination of promise and peril—a challenge almost without precedent.

Protestants thus experienced California's social-cultural landscape as a kind of threshold of dual possibilities. It could become a New Babylon or a New Eden. Whichever direction it took, California probably seemed to most Protestants, in the words of United Brethren Clergyman Marion R. Drury in 1908, "a different civilization from that found east of the Rocky Mountains." The following chapters describe how Protestants west of the Rockies have tried to influence this Pacific Coast civilization.

SUGGESTED FURTHER READING:

Ernst, Eldon G. "American religious history from a Pacific Coast perspective," chapter 1 in Carl Guarneri and David Alvarez, eds., *Religion and Society in the American West: Historical Essays*. Lanham, Md.: University Press of America, 1987.

Frankiel, Sandra Sizer. "California and the Southwest," in C.H. Lippy and P.W. Williams, eds., *Encyclopedia of the American Religious Experience*. New York: Charles Scribners's Sons, 1988.

Lane, Belden C. *Landscapes of the Sacred: Geography and Narrative in American Spirituality*. New York: Paulist Press, 1988.

Lantis, Davis W., Steiner, Rodney, and Karinen, Arthur. *California, Land of Contrast*. Dubuque, Iowa: Kendall/Hunt, 1981.

Limbaugh, Ronald H. "The nature of John Muir's religion," *Pacific Historian* 29 (1985).

Lustig, Jess, guest ed. *Envisioning California*, special issue of *California History* LXVIII (1989-90).

Mead, Sidney E. *The Lively Experiment: The Shaping of Christianity in America*. New York: Harper and Row, 1963.

McWilliams, Carey. *Southern California Country, An Island on the Land*. New York: Duell, Sloan and Pearce, 1946.

Nadeau, Remi. *California: The New Society*. New York: D. McKay Co., 1963.

Nash, Roderick. *Wilderness and the American Mind*. New Haven, Ct.: Yale University Press, 1973.

Richardson, E. Allen. *Strangers in This Land: Pluralism and the Response to Diversity in the United States*. New York: The Pilgrim Press, 1988.

Whitaker, Robert. "Is California Irreligious?" *Sunset Magazine* 16 (1906).

Wollenberg, Charles. *Golden Gate Metropolis: Perspectives on Bay Area History*. Berkeley: Institute of Governmental Studies, University of California, 1985.

4 The Protestant Impact on California: The Formative Period, 1850-1920

In the year 1913, former Methodist minister H. Stitt Wilson wrote a "Letter to Berkeley Socialists: Declining the Nomination for the Mayorality of Berkeley (Second Term)," published in his volume entitled *The Harlots and Pharisees: or, the Barbary Coast in a Barbarous Land*. Having served a two-year term as Berkeley's mayor, Wilson was ready to return to the public platform where since 1901 he had preached social reform with a progressive Protestant flavor up and down the state with great popularity. Wilson preached his social-religious vision with Methodist fervor, writing on one occasion that "the greatest need of the world—and of our own California . . . is a spiritual and ethical revival, an awakening and education of the social conscience." On another occasion he preached that "except this civilization be born again we cannot enter the next phase of the Kingdom of God."

H. Stitt Wilson had moved to California from Chicago. As a young student in the early 1890s he had been drawn into what became known as the social gospel movement. The social gospel referred to Protestant ministers, editors and writers, and educators who sought to re-orient Christian theology and mission to meet the social problems that emerged with late nineteenth-century industrialism and urbanization. They criticized traditional American economic competitive individualism that seemed to be based on human greed and to have fostered increasing poverty and oppression among the working classes. They called for social reconstruction of society by church and state alike, and the more radical of these reformers advocated programs and philosophies commonly identified as "Christian Socialism."

As a social gospel activist, Berkeley's Mayor Wilson simply was carrying into the early twentieth-century years of American progressive reformism the long-established Protestant aspiration to influence the formation of a "righteous society." The public Protestant impulse in California had developed over a seventy-year period of vigorous activity and organization, with somewhat different successes and failures in the northern and southern regions of the state. Though conditions in both regions were to change dramatically after the turn of the century, regional distinctions had been set and patterns of Protestant influence had taken foundational shape during the later nineteenth-century decades.

Nineteenth-Century Foundations

The Protestant impact on California's developing social formation and cultural ethos took foundational shape in the San Francisco Bay Area where population centers first emerged. This new and rapidly growing social environment, cosmopolitan and ethnically diverse from its beginning, presented an unprecedented challenge to most Protestants accustomed to representing the nation's dominant cultural-religious heritage. Unlike the rest of the nation, however, the majority of the Bay Area populace identified with no religious institution, thereby encouraging a secular tone to public life. Moreover, the religiously-affiliated minority represented a wide plurality of faith traditions, none of which enjoyed a position of predominance by virtue of size or social position. Roman Catholics, in fact, far outnumbered Protestants among church-related Californians. Nevertheless, conscious of their minority position, California Protestants vigorously strove to influence this Pacific region of American civilization in ways compatible with the goals, methods, and emphases inherited and brought from other parts of the nation.

Local Churches

The American Protestant goal of molding a Christian society in nineteenth-century California depended first of all on vital local churches. Here was the traditional primary religious link between peoples' private and public lives. Public worship in the church's sanctuary, especially pulpit preaching, commonly linked Christian beliefs and teachings to the conditions and events of the civil order. Church programs of religious education, fellowship and recreation, and ministry to personal needs within the congregation were meant to nourish family life in the home, to model community life and to produce moral and enlightened citizens for society-at-large. Churches were supposed to equip persons spiritually and morally to influence and "uplift" the secular contexts of their daily lives.

The churches' mission included evangelism—programs reaching out to the unchurched with the goal of influencing their lives spiritually as well as materially, always with the possibility of bringing them into church affiliation as well. Ideally evangelism would increase the size and number of churches, thereby expanding their influence in the social environment. Many churches also became centers of social services in their neighborhoods, offering programs to meet a variety of human needs. From the 1850s on, therefore, more and more Protestant churches dotted the rapidly-growing California social landscape, first in the San Francisco Bay Area and soon in the Los Angeles region, contributing to the shaping of individual lives and to some extent the society within which those individuals lived.

With local church congregations as their primary social center of ongoing cultivation of religious culture, Protestants also reached out with specialized programs and organizations to influence life outside of their local church buildings. They concentrated their efforts most effectively in the areas of education, printed mass media, and benevolent social services and reform advocacy.

Education

Second only to congregational worship, the educational enterprise energized and nourished nineteenth-century Protestant church-related life in California and contributed to the state's cultural formation. The people's biblical literacy and reasoned knowledge of their faith were essential to most Protestant concepts of a healthy church. Likewise, a sound social order, especially a democratic republic, depended upon an educated and morally enlightened people. From the earliest years, therefore, California Protestants created and supported schools ranging from the earliest grade levels through high school to colleges and graduate schools of the highest level.

Protestants overwhelmingly supported public education as it developed, falteringly at first, in California during the 1850s. Unlike in most eastern areas of the United States, San Francisco public schools received Catholic as well as Protestant support during the early years. By the 1880s, however, public schools had assumed a distinctively Protestant flavor in curricula and customs before they became increasingly secularized after the turn of the century. Some denominations, notably Episcopalians, Lutherans, and Christian Reformed (Dutch), established their own parochial schools, most of which eventually closed unable to compete with the expanding and strengthening public school system.

The Protestant impact on higher education in California was profound and far-reaching, despite the fact that many of the originally church-related colleges and universities eventually distanced themselves from their denominational associations. The earliest of these schools appeared in the north. Congregationalists and Presbyterians were instrumental in the 1855 founding of the College of California in Oakland, which later moved to Berkeley and in 1868 became the first State University (now the University of California, Berkeley). Mills College for women in Oakland (chartered in 1885) and Stanford University (1891) both began with strong Protestant input, though neither developed denominational connections. Of more enduring denominational identity was the present-day University of the Pacific in Stockton, founded in Santa Clara as a Methodist college in 1851.

Most of the enduring colleges and universities with denominational origins, however, were established in Southern California during the late nineteenth-early twentieth century where Protestantism was becoming a powerful regional cultural force producing one of the nation's centers of private higher education. Among these prominent schools are the University of Southern California in Los Angeles (Methodist), Chapman College (Disciples of Christ), Pomona College in Claremont (Congregational), Occidental College in Los Angeles (Presbyterian), Whittier College (Quaker), the University of Redlands (Baptist), and Loma Linda University (Seventh-Day Adventist).

At the same time, Protestants concentrated their programs in theological education for church leadership at the graduate professional level in the San Francisco-Berkeley Bay Area. In 1866 the Congregationalists founded the first enduring Protestant theological seminary in the western United States in San Francisco (moving to Oakland in 1870 and to Berkeley in 1901) known since 1916 as Pacific School of Religion (originally Pacific Theological Seminary), an independent interdenominational school. The Presbyterians founded San Francisco Theological Seminary in 1871, now located fifteen miles north of the Golden Gate in San Anselmo. In 1890 the Baptists began theological education in Oakland, moving soon to Berkeley with the present-day American Baptist Seminary of the West. When the Episcopalians in 1893 established their Church Divinity School of the Pacific, and the Unitarians in 1904 opened their School for the Ministry (now called Starr King School for the Ministry), the Bay Area became the major center of Protestant theological education in the United States west of Chicago.

The Printed Mass Media

In conjunction with educational enterprises, the printed mass media became a second means by which Protestants made a foundational impact on California life and thought. Protestants always had been a people of the written word, rooted essentially in the Bible as the source for expounding Christian theology and practice. Publishing and circulating printed material for the promotion of Christian knowledge and commitment long pre-dated Protestant entry into mid-nineteenth-century California. American Bible, tract, and publication societies organized on the East Coast early in the century quickly appeared in California during Gold Rush years (The California Bible Society began in 1849). From then on these organizations, plus similar denominational agencies, reached people in every imaginable location distributing Bibles and various types of religious literature. Perhaps most instrumental in relating Protestant concerns to the broad expression of California social-cultural life and thought, however, were denominational newspapers.

Church-related publishing naturally followed the familiar regional pattern of development. Most newspapers were based in the San Francisco Bay Area and circulated outward to surrounding towns, until by the turn of the century they were linked to the burgeoning Los Angeles area that had become a second publishing center. The Christian Churches (Disciples of Christ), for example, published at least nine different newspapers in Northern California before *The Christian Messenger* became statewide in 1918. A few years later *The Unified Informer* became a Southern California-based

Disciples of Christ periodical. *The California Christian Advocate* was the first denominational newspaper of long duration, published by the Methodists beginning in 1851 and lasting until 1932. Other major nineteenth-century California newspapers lasting several decades were published by the Congregationalists (*The Pacific*), The Presbyterians (*The Occident*), and the Episcopalians (*Pacific Churchman*, which celebrated the 100th anniversary of its continual publication in 1966).

These denominationally-produced periodicals featured news and commentary not only on the churches and specifically religious matters but also on social, political, economic, and cultural issues of California life generally and frequently of the nation and world. The varieties of racial-ethnic groups whom the churches represented and to whom they ministered found visibility in these denominational publications. They carried news articles, editorials, reviews of books and magazines and public cultural events, prose and poetry as well as sermons, devotional pieces, and moral-theological essays. These denominational newspapers thus served as a primary means through which California Protestants communicated widely both among themselves and to the general reading public. Through them Protestants recalled their histories and projected their ambitions, publicized their ongoing life and special events, and expressed their ideas and opinions as individual citizens and as churches.

Equally important, these denominational newspapers helped maintain a connecting link between California churches in the West and their denominational networks centered in the eastern United States. As such they fostered among their churches a larger Pacific regional consciousness—the edge of the American West on the Pacific Coast from Mexico to British Columbia. Some denominational newspapers directly connected California to the greater Pacific Far West—*The Pacific Baptist, The Pacific Unitarian, The Pacific Friend* (Quaker), and others. The *Pacific Churchman* (Episcopal), for example, carried regular reports from Dioceses of Oregon, Washington (Olympia), Utah, and Arizona, as well as from Los Angeles, Sacramento, and San Francisco (its place of publication).

Conscious of being as close to Asia as to Europe, denominational newspapers also helped California churches maintain contact with mission activity throughout the world. Articles and editorials on social-political as well as religious events and conditions in nations around the world commonly set contexts for church foreign mission news and discussion. Those who regularly read these newspapers must have added a rather sophisticated international awareness to their California church environment.

It is impossible to weigh with any accuracy just how influential nineteenth-century California Protestant journalism was on the public-at-large. However, altogether these newspapers circulated widely among church-related persons throughout the State for many years. They represented a wide variety of interests, perspectives, and opinions of a significant part of California's religiously-connected population. At times these newspapers could record and promote interests widely-held by Protestants nationally as well as in the state, such as the campaigns for temperance and prohibition. Because they consistently touched on most aspects of California life, and because they were informative and at times persuasive in debated issues (though by no means uniform in positions taken on controversial matters), they no doubt were read outside of church circles as well. They provided one important means by which California's sub-regional cultures interacted during their formative years, thereby contributing to a California state consciousness. They also countered a California provincialism by interacting with the larger Pacific Far West, with the eastern United States, and with other nations of the world.

In other words, because California Protestant churches identified themselves with national and worldwide religious traditions and institutional networks, their journalistic expressions contributed to the state's conscious linkage to life and thought beyond its own borders. Conversely, because the churches ministered to immigrants of many nationalities, their journalistic expressions contributed to California's public consciousness of the plurality of cultures thriving within its own borders.

Social Service and Reform

By mid-nineteenth century the American Protestant aspirations for a Christian democratic republic had led them into a maze of campaigns for humanitarian and moral goals. Evangelical revivals stimulated the moral sensitivity of great crowds, and like political rallies, garnered support for benevolent and reform causes. Voluntary societies raised money and workers to help implement the agenda of social betterment projects. Especially in industrializing cities, unhealthy living and working conditions produced growing numbers of the poor and needy. Schools, hospitals, orphanages, and prisons received charitable attention and widespread popular Protestant support, as did campaigns for temperance and Sabbath observance. More controversial were movements passionately advocating greater civil rights for women and the abolition of human slavery—issues reaching the heart of constitutional guarantees of life, liberty, and the pursuit of happiness. All of these concerns came to California as Protestant church leaders determined to extend their national social vision to the Pacific.

Even before denominations established stable parish structures, Protestant social mission organizations took hold in the early San Francisco Bay Area. A good example is the Young Men's Christian Association (YMCA), which began work there in 1853. Originally a program to assist young men migrating to cities with lodging and meals, recreational activities, and vocational training, the YMCA soon expanded its benevolent mission to reach the whole community of human needs. It raised money and stimulated volunteers to support rescue missions and charitable organizations. Being closely in touch with churches, the YMCA also fostered Protestant piety and evangelistic outreach outside of church walls by organizing Bible-study groups, distributing religious literature, preaching on street corners, and promoting citywide revival campaigns. By 1880 the Young Women's Christian Association (YWCA) had begun similar work directed especially to the special needs of women, and during the following decade both organizations began similar work in Los Angeles. The Y's thus paved the way for the churches' social orientation and impact on California's urban centers and surrounding towns.

The churches themselves quickly jumped into the arena of pressing social needs, as exemplified by the Episcopal Church Diocese of California. In 1869 the Diocese founded the Church Home Association to care for poor, aged, and disabled women, and to provide temporary residence for women seeking employment. St. Luke's Hospital was founded two years later in San Francisco. San Mateo became the site of the Armitage Orphanage for boys and the Maria Kip Orphanage for girls. Church-related schools such as St. Matthew's School for boys and Irving Institute for girls complemented and competed with the developing public school system. The Guild of St. Barnabas for nurses, the Seaman's Institute in San

Francisco, the John Tennant Memorial Home in Pacific Grove, and the St. Dorothy's Rest in Sonoma were flourishing charitable institutions that made an impact on the community-at-large. Meanwhile San Francisco's Cathedral of the Good Samaritan typified the urban Protestant "Institutional Church" that met community needs with a reading room, a gymnasium, a medical dispensary and clinic, a nursery, and clubs and classes for all ages.

Few could quarrel with these kinds of benevolent activities, but many did counter Protestants' attempts to impose their moral commitments on the public by means of social pressure and political legislation. The movements for temperance and for Sabbath observance best illustrate this Protestant social dynamic.

The temperance movement to curb the consumption of alcoholic beverages long had been at the core of American Protestant moral reform aspirations. (The American Temperance Society began in Boston in 1826.) Alcohol abuse was seen as the primary vice infecting all of life. Drunkenness led to violence and moral decay (especially gambling and sexual vices), to broken homes, ineffective (or loss of) employment, and irresponsible political citizenship. Saloons where people congregated to drink and socialize became identified as almost the antithesis of local churches. Churches, therefore, battled against saloons.

Temperance crusades drew strong support from women, who commonly suffered harsh consequences of alcoholic drunkenness among men upon whose economic support home life depended. With the formation of the national Women's Christian Temperance Union (WCTU) in the early 1870s, organized in California in 1879, their temperance concerns became connected to a variety of social reformist causes, not the least being women's suffrage. Women came to believe that the evils of alcohol and accompanying vices would require political action, and women's votes would help secure moral legislation. By the 1890s the WCTU had brought enough pressure to bear on public opinion and politicians, supported widely by Protestant churches, to help effect some modest prohibitionist legislation both in Berkeley and in Los Angeles. But these and other moral reform efforts drew opposition in the secular and religiously pluralistic social environment of California. By the turn of the century, political action for controversial social causes would become divisive even among Protestants themselves.

Meanwhile, Protestants had pursued their even greater commitment to promoting and preserving their sacred day, Sunday, in California society. At the very least, Protestants thought, their moral influence might succeed in keeping the Sabbath free of vice-ridden activities within the public civil order.

Strict Sabbath observance (Sabbatarianism) had characterized Anglo-American Protestantism since its transplantation from old to New England with seventeenth-century Puritans. Most Christians historically had observed the Old Testament Hebrew Sabbath (the seventh day ordained for rest from normal life activity and for worship) on Sunday. In the Puritan Reformation, Sabbath observance represented the glorification of God in church and society— the binding of church practice and civil law to produce a righteous society. In nineteenth-century America, Sabbath observance bonded Anglo Protestant denominations in their attempt to mold the nation's cultural ethos and social environment. People were to abstain from work and recreation in order to concentrate on corporate worship of God and on spiritual reflection and nourishment. Church leaders helped secure Sabbath laws in most states, which specifically prohibited business and labor enterprise, organized recreation (theater, games, saloons, etc.), and even travel. Sabbath laws symbolized the depth and scope of Protestant influence in the civil order.

In nineteenth-century California, however, Sabbath laws were foreign to the Hispanic heritage and not of interest to many of the people flooding into gold mining communities. To Protestant church leaders, securing Sabbath legislation became a primary objective toward the goal of bringing their vision of moral order to this otherwise secular and diverse cultural environment. Their early social-political advocacy succeeded, temporarily, when in 1858 the Legislature passed modest Sabbath legislation that lasted twenty-five years. But widespread public indifference and lack of observance, lax government enforcement, and opposition from both secular and other religious groups, led finally to permanent repeal in 1883. California thus became the first state to repeal Sabbath laws entirely, setting a trend followed by many eastern states during the next decade.

From this experience California Protestants discovered both the possibilities and limitations of their collective influence on the customs and ethos of public life. As the *Pacific Churchman* editorialized in 1900, they had made little headway in San Francisco:

The average Christian citizen scarcely realizes how imperiled is the sanctity of the Lord's day in San Francisco. Only by eternal vigilance and prompt moral suasion or legal procedure can the lax tendency to keep this day be checked. . . . The stranger visiting our city is astonished to find the corner groceries and saloons, the ice-cream parlors, photograph galleries and in some parts of the city, the music halls and shooting galleries doing a thriving business all day Sunday, often under the shadow of our churches.

Under the shadow of churches, too, was a far greater obstacle to a moral social environment. Major disabilities suffered by black people in nineteenth-century America were present also on the California frontier, where white racism extended to Chinese immigrants and Hispanic *Californios* as well. Protestants took both sides in these people's struggles for their basic civil rights. Black church leaders such as Methodist clergymen J.J. Moore, J.B. Sanderson, and T.M.D. Ward took strong leadership roles among black Californians seeking equal benefits of education, medical care, housing, judicial appeal, and political suffrage. Some Chinese and Japanese Protestant clergy likewise tried to find ways to help relieve their people's oppression, receiving support from some Anglo mission leaders. The Anglo mainline denominations offered charitable services to oppressed racial minority people, and their newspapers often promoted their cause for social justice. But the California social environment remained far more hospitable to white citizens than to the diverse peoples of color in their midst. Churches, like most other institutions and activities, moreover, remained racially segregated.

The Progressive Era: 1900-1920

In the first two decades of the twentieth century, California public life witnessed currents of "progressive" social and cultural change that engaged Protestant citizens and their churches. Protestant institutions of education and publication, for example, experienced significant modification. Colleges and seminaries began to feel the impact of the secular academic standards, research orientation, and scientific methods. Denominational periodicals gradually found their earlier function as sources of religious commentary on matters of public interest eroded by modern urban daily newspapers, whose professional staffs of journalists could win readers with a breadth of coverage.

While education and media were undergoing these changes, however, California Protestants heightened their involvement in the state's movements for progressive reform. Their activities, and degrees of success, took somewhat divergent paths in the two metropolitan areas of the North and the South.

Regional Expressions

From 1907-1911 much of the Bay Area Protestant community became caught up in the attempt to remove the Union Labor Party administration in San Francisco. In 1907, following investigations by a reformist newspaper into the wheelings and dealings of Mayor Eugene Schmitz and his political associates, court proceedings for graft were initiated. The reformist-minded Protestant press and many lay and clerical church leaders rallied behind the prosecution. "We are having a true revival of religion," wrote Presbyterian minister William Rader about the cause; "God is moving the city, and when a number of our supervisors and other officials are sent to prison we will be more free." For a time, the reformers kept the Union Labor Party out of the city government, but the legal proceedings bogged down by 1909, the Union Party won back the city elective offices that same year, and Protestants had to be content with their relative powerlessness over San Francisco politics and public opinion.

The situation was different in Los Angeles, where Anglo Protestants wielded greater public power. Believing their city to be an "ideal Protestant city" and a "model Christian community," church leaders did not find it necessary to battle against the political power of the kinds of laboring and non-Protestant groups that carried the day in San Francisco. Charter reform passed in 1903, with significant Protestant support, making Los Angeles the first American city with the initiative, referendum, and recall (progressive landmarks). Congregationalist John R. Haynes, a medical doctor with wealth from both his practice and his real estate dealings, was an outspoken Protestant social reformer. His Good Government Association targeted the political influence of the Southern Pacific Railroad in the city in 1905, but upon investigation, it found little in the city administration that needed cleansing. Haynes had to acknowledge that, while city officials were not as efficient and professional as he would like, they were "good and decent men."

Statewide Impact

By 1910, Protestant-rooted social reform was ready to move from the local to the state level. That year the race for governor was particularly heated, and Protestants were in the thick of the battle. Political reformism was on the upsurge. Bearing the brunt of the political fire was the Southern Pacific Railroad, a huge corporation that monopolized much of the state's transportation and thus wielded great economic and political power in the pursuit of its business interests.

Protestants figured in the election in at least two ways. First, the rhetoric of reform had an unmistakable tone of Protestant revivalism. The label "progressive" had come to mean democratic reform against corruption in government and big business. For many it also meant combining a Protestant-flavored moral reform of the public civil order with the most enlightened knowledge and expertise available from modern social science and professional leadership. Progressive politics took on a crusading spirit for social righteousness that was familiar to most Protestants, though they did not agree among themselves on many of the particular issues and proposed solutions.

Second, some of the candidates in 1910 had direct Protestant ties. Albert J. Wallace, for example, the Republican candidate for lieutenant governor, was a former Methodist clergyman who later had prospered in business (agriculture and oil interests). His Southern California ties were expected to gain that region's Protestant votes for the party ticket that featured the North's Hiram Johnson as its gubernatorial candidate. Wallace also was president of the California Anti-Saloon League, a political organization of the larger prohibition movement that long had received widespread Protestant support.

One opponent of the Johnson-Wallace ticket was J. Stitt Wilson, the former Methodist minister and soon-to-be mayor of Berkeley. Stitt was the Socialist Party's candidate for governor in 1910. Wilson and the Socialists, along with the Democratic candidates, lost the 1910 election to Johnson and Wallace, due in part to the strength of the Southern California Protestant votes.

In addition to general Protestant support of Hiram Johnson's progressive Republican administration, two moral issues of special concern to the Anglo-American religious community in California rose to prominence. Temperance, we have seen, had been a traditional Protestant issue in California, led by the WCTU. During the progressive era, however, a newer organization, essentially political, took over the leadership of the movement for legal prohibition. Southern California, with its strong Protestant community, became the state's stronghold of prohibitionist sentiment. Northern California Protestants, while strong in some rural and small town areas and in the Bay Area city of Berkeley, were continually frustrated in their attempts to impose prohibition in San Francisco and the wine-making regions north of the Bay Area. Protestants were thus unable to push the state into the "dry" column, despite the WCTU's success in leading the passage of women's suffrage in 1911. Not until national prohibition was passed at the close of World War I did California, along with the rest of the Nation, experience the ban on alcohol.

The other major reform issue in which California Protestants played a leading role was in the forcing of prostitution underground. In 1914, a "red-light abatement" initiative was approved. The WCTU spearheaded the campaign, building on the recent franchisement of women and newly arisen concerns over venereal disease as a threat to public health. By 1920 California Protestants thus had a sense of hard won victory in asserting a least some of their aspirations for influence on California society.

Victory, though, came with irony. Californians had become preoccupied with the World War, especially when the United States entered the battle in 1917. With few public dissenters, Protestants joined others in approving the nation's action. Participation in the war, and the hope of social reconstruction of the postwar world, became the climax of American Protestant crusades. But it soon would become clear that a new era had dawned in California, as in the nation as a whole, dashing any realistic hopes for Protestant dominance of the public culture and the civil order. Not only had Protestants become aware of their loss of national hegemony as religious pluralism began to come-of-age and secularity increased, but they no longer could ignore internal divisions developing within their own religious community. California, moreover, was on the forefront of these nationwide developments.

Growing Division Among California Protestants

In order to understand the larger scope of Protestant formative impact on California's social-cultural environment, it remains to note the emerging division within Protestantism itself during the turn-of-the century decades. This division might best be understood as divergent responses to late nineteenth-century modern social and intellectual challenges to religious life and thought—challenges to traditional orthodox theology and practice. The labels "liberal" and "conservative" are too imprecise to describe adequately the variety and complexity of these responses to modernity, but they are generally accurate historical references of the age that distinguish these two unfolding religious orientations.

Protestant liberalism, or the "new theology," reinterpreted and reformulated traditional doctrines in light of new scientific theories and knowledge, such as Darwin's evolutionary theory and its application to human life. Liberals also applied modern critical scholarship to the Scriptures, which allowed them to analyze texts for historical, linguistic, and archeological accuracy and to reinterpret passages for their moral and spiritual meaning as well as their literal translation. Likewise the "social gospel" attempted to locate societal implications of theology with the help of the new social sciences, attempting to redirect the churches' mission toward the reform and reconstruction of urban-industrial society. In short, liberals tried to make Christianity relevant and persuasive to modern life and thought.

Many denominations establishing themselves in the late nineteenth-century California urban frontier expressed various aspects of these liberalizing tendencies in their public worship, in their schools and publications, and in their programs of social outreach. During the early twentieth century, these progressive reforms became part of conventional denominational life and institutions. Through local and regional federations of churches, moreover, these denominations gained a sense of strength in their shared progressive Protestant identity and in their cooperative social-religious presence in the larger community.

But not all were comfortable with these changes taking place in conventional church life. Conservative responses to liberal theological and social innovations, and to new approaches to biblical interpretation, began to grow. Some feared that the supernatural was being lost in humanistic and naturalistic redefinitions of Christian life and thought. Others became disaffected from conventional church life that seemed lacking in spiritual vitality and moral discipline. To them the founding of church federations only enhanced the threat of apostasy and its influence in society. Conservatives wanted to protect the faith from the "acids of modernity," the corruption of secular life and thought.

Most denominations managed to contain both the liberal and the conservative tendencies within their churches during the late nineteenth and early twentieth-century decades. But slowly the cracks of division widened. Periodic conflicts over the content of sermons, published books, and school curricula erupted. The more extreme opponents of liberalism in church life then began to coalesce into conferences, movements, and alternative institutions separate from traditional denominational associations. They stressed the preservation of biblically-grounded doctrinal orthodoxy, and moral and spiritual revival. Out of these movements emerged a whole new wing of American Protestantism at the dawn of the twentieth century that came to include the fundamentalist, holiness, and pentecostal churches. They found in Southern California as congenial an environment for growth, nourishment, and public expression as had the more conventional denominational churches in the several decades before.

The roots of twentieth-century fundamentalism reach back to nineteenth-century issues of biblical authority in Christian theology and practice. Darwin's theory of biological evolution forced the issue because it seemed to contradict the biblical account of creation and its supernatural design, especially in relation to human development. Scholars who studied the Bible "scientifically" (critically) questioned the divine inspiration of the Bible's authors whose words apparently conflicted with modern historical and scientific knowledge. As church pulpits, college classrooms, and publications increasingly reflected this liberal approach to the Bible, resistance mounted among some Protestants and a counter-offensive emerged consciously opposing theological accommodation to the modern intellectual climate.

The new conservative movement took extreme concrete form in "prophetic" Bible conferences that appeared regularly beginning in the mid-1870s. These conferences rallied support for biblical "inerrancy"—the infallible literal accuracy of the scriptures and the "verbal inspiration" of their authors. The absolute authority of the Bible in all of life thus would be preserved. Orthodox doctrine was affirmed on biblical grounds, especially Christ's divinity revealed in his virgin birth, his miraculous works, his death that atoned for the sins of believers, and his bodily resurrection and predicted second coming to earth. Prophecy specifically applied biblical texts to human history. Dispensationalists (dispensations mean historical periods of supernatural revelation) formulated prophetic views in which human history is preordained by God to culminate in the "pre-millennial" (before the thousand-year reign) return of Christ.

These prophetic Bible conferences led to the founding of Bible institutes to train teachers and missionaries in the faith untouched by liberal ideas. The famous revival evangelist Dwight L. Moody (who campaigned in San Francisco in the 1880s) established a Bible institute in Chicago that became a model for dozens of other such schools throughout the nation. It still thrives. In like fashion, the Bible Institute of Los Angeles (BIOLA, now Biola College), founded largely by the efforts of wealthy oil businessman Lyman Stewart in 1908, became the most influential center of conservative fundamentalist Protestantism west of Chicago.

Lyman Stewart, a long-time lay leader in Southern California Presbyterianism, was a staunch opponent of liberal influences in the churches. His vision for BIOLA was a strong alternative to California's established colleges and seminaries, which he viewed as dangerously liberal. Stewart also helped finance a series, written by various conservative theologians, of twelve small volumes together entitled *The Fundamentals*, published in 1910-1915. These were widely disseminated among Protestants throughout the nation and provided the basis of the current label "fundamentalist."

Southern California also became a center of two other emerging conservative Protestant movements whose primary concerns differed from, but were in sympathy with, the priorities of biblical fundamentalism. These were the closely related Holiness and Pentecostal movements that emphasized moral discipline and spiritual experience. The holiness movement arose primarily within mid-nineteenth-century Methodism among those who felt that the conventional churches had lost touch with John Wesley's emphasis on personal moral discipline and sanctification. Holiness revivals eventually led people out of the established churches to form new sectarian communities and finally such new denominations as the Salvation Army, the Christian and Missionary Alliance, and, in 1895, the Church of the Nazarene in Los Angeles.

Independent holiness churches began to appear in Los Angeles during the 1880s. Holiness Christians also began to ally with disaf-

fected conservative Protestants from other than Methodist denominations for evangelistic revivals. With the founding of the Church
of the Nazarene by ex-Methodist minister Phineas F.
Bresee in
1895, a new holiness denomination was born. During the next
twenty years Bresee led the Nazarenes to remarkable growth in
California through the formation of churches, the periodical
Nazarene Messenger, evangelistic programs, and the Pacific Bible
College in Los Angeles.

Closely related to the holiness revival, the pentecostal movement emphasized the spiritual experience of faith healing and outward emotional expression through the speaking in unknown
tongues—"baptism in the Holy Spirit." Pentecostalism refers to the
early church's experience of Pentecost as recorded in Acts 2:4,
including the prophecy that similar spiritual manifestations would
occur just prior to Christ's second coming. An early expression of
the movement in modern times occurred in the 1906 Azusa Street
revival in Los Angeles led by itinerant black church preacher
William Seymour. The Azusa Street Mission attracted nationwide
attention and contributed greatly to the spread of Pentecostal
preaching and the eventual formation of new denominations such
as the Assemblies of God, The Church of God, and, in California
after World War I, the International Church of the Foursquare
Gospel founded by Aimee Semple McPherson.

Altogether the rising fundamentalist, Holiness, and Pentecostal
movements represented a formidable alternative to the established
mainline denominations. As they gained solid footing in Southern
California during the early twentieth century, they hoped to revitalize and redirect the churches' life and moral influence in California society.

The interrelationship of these movements can well be seen in
Northern California's revivalist leader of the Christian and Missionary Alliance, Carrie Judd Montgomery. In 1890 she settled in
Oakland, began holding weekly prayer and healing meetings,
founded the Home for Peace (spiritual and physical healing) in
1893, an orphanage in 1895, and the periodical *Triumph of Faith*. In
1908 she received the "baptism of the Spirit," and in 1914 she was a
major force behind a worldwide Pentecostal Camp Meeting held at
Cazadero, just north of San Francisco on the Russian River.

By 1914, then, as the Great War in Europe was about to alter the
course of world and national history, the formative period of

Protestantism in California's still-young society came to an end on a divisive note. In the years ahead their divergent commitments would significantly affect preaching and public worship, what was taught in colleges, the involvement of churches in social and political issues, and the messages communicated through public mass media. Overall, Protestant disputes over the relationship of theology to science and social betterment would diffuse into the modern secular culture. It soon became clear to California Protestants that a new era had dawned in their Pacific Coast pilgrimage.

SUGGESTED FURTHER READING:

Anderson, Douglas Firth. " 'We have here a different civilization':
  Protestant identity in the San Francisco Bay Area, 1906-1909,"
  Western Historical Quarterly 23 (May 1992).

Engh, Michael E., S.J. *Frontier Faiths: Church, Temple, and Synagogue in
  Los Angeles 1846-1888.* Albuquerque: University of New Mexico
  Press, 1992.

Frankiel, Sandra Sizer. *California's Spiritual Frontiers: Religious
  Alternatives in Anglo-Protestantism, 1850-1910.* Berkeley: University
  of California Press, 1988.

Hopkins, Charles Howard. *The Rise of the Social Gospel in American
  Protestantism 1864-1915.* New Haven, Ct.: Yale University Press,
  1940.

Hutchison, William R. *The Modernist Impulse in American Protestantism.*
  Cambridge: Harvard University Press, 1976.

Marsden, George. *Fundamentalism and American Culture: The Shaping of
  Twentieth-Century Evangelicalism, 1870-1925.* New York: Oxford
  University Press, 1980.

Mowry, George E. *The California Progressives.* Berkeley: University of
  California Press, 1951.

Murphy, Larry G. "A balm in Gilead: Black churches and the thrust for
  civil rights in California, 1850-1880," chapter 12 in Carl Guarneri
  and David Alvarez, eds., *Religion and Society in the American West:
  Historical Essays.* Lanham, Md.: University Press of America, 1987.

Singleton, Gregory H. *Religion in the City of Angels: American Protestant
  Culture and Urbanization, Los Angeles, 1850-1930.* Ann Arbor, Mich.:
  UMI Research Press, 1979.

Starr, Kevin. *Americans and the California Dream, 1850-1915.* New York:
  Oxford University Press, 1973.

Synan, Vinson. *The Holiness-Pentecostal Movement in the United States.*
  Grand Rapids, Mich.: William B. Eerdmans, 1971.

Szasz, Ferenc M. *The Divided Mind of Protestant America, 1880-1930.*
  University, Alabama: University of Alabama Press, 1982.

Weber, Timothy P. *Living in the Shadow of the Second Coming: American
  Premillennialism, 1875-1925.* New York: Oxford University Press,
  1979.

5 Protestant Diversity in California Culture: The Middle Period, 1920 to 1960

In December of 1918, just at the close of World War I, a large outdoor banner on the 4,000-seat Los Angeles Philharmonic Auditorium advertised "Aimee Semple McPherson—Lady Evangelist—Nightly 7:30 P.M. Full orchestra, Choir, Holy Ghost Revival." Before overflowing crowds, Sister Aimee (1890-1944) began her Los Angeles career that would bring her national fame unmatched before or since by a California Protestant church personality.

"I bring spiritual consolation to the middle class," she once characterized her ministry, "leaving those above to themselves and those below to the Salvation Army." Born in Canada as Aimee Elizabeth Kennedy and raised on a small, unpretentious farm, she knew "those below" through her mother's regular participation in Salvation Army services in nearby Ingersoll, Ontario, services she too attended. She passed from the Holiness community to Pentecostalism through the ministry of Robert James Semple, an Irish-born boilermaker turned earnest evangelist, whom she left high school to marry in 1908. The Semples traveled to Hong Kong, intending to work together as Pentecostal missionaries, but Robert died of malaria. After returning to the United States in 1910, Aimee married an American wholesale grocer named Harold Stewart McPherson (who divorced her in 1921). Meanwhile, between 1911 and 1918 she gained experience as an evangelist and faith healer, traversing the eastern United States and conducting services in rented quarters and tents.

In December, 1918 she arrived in Los Angeles, where she decided to make her home, though she continued to travel widely as a Pentecostal revivalist for the next four years. In 1922 she began to speak of the "foursquare gospel"—Jesus Christ as Savior, Baptizer in the Holy Spirit, Healer, and Coming King. On January 1, 1923, she dedicated her 5,300-seat Angelus Temple in the then-growing Echo Park section of Los Angeles, having raised over $300,000 to see it through to completion. That same year, she founded a Bible school that by 1926 had been renamed the Lighthouse for International Foursquare Evangelism (LIFE) Bible College, housed in a separate building.

With the completion of Angelus Temple, Sister Aimee traveled far less than she had previously, but she found a new way to reach those who did not come to her. In 1924 she opened radio station KFSG to carry "Cathedral of the Air" broadcasts, thereby becoming the first woman to be licensed by the Federal Communications Commission to operate a radio station. In 1927 this radio station was joined with the Bible college, the publishing house, the Angelus Temple Commissary (which dispensed food and clothing to any who applied—during the Depression of the 1930s, over a million people may have been helped) and incorporated as the International Church of the Foursquare Gospel (ICFG). By the end of the decade the now international denomination had held its sixth annual convention at Angelus Temple, which featured a music department of several bands, orchestras, organists, pianists, quartets, choirs, glee clubs, and many soloists.

At Sister Aimee's death in 1944, her denomination had some 22,000 members in over 400 churches in North America and some 200 mission stations elsewhere. In 1986, the denomination, headed by Aimee's son Rolf, claimed over one million members worldwide, 188,757 of them in the United States.

Aimee Semple McPherson and her institutional legacy in California express several significant characteristics of twentieth-century California Protestantism. First, as an immigrant to the Golden State, she highlights the importance that immigration has had in Protestant developments. Immigration had been decisive in setting the course of California society in the nineteenth century. Who came from where, and in what strength, and in what part of the state they settled, remained important questions in the twentieth century for determining Protestant impact in California life. Sister Aimee was but one of tens of thousands of Protestants who succumbed to the allure of Southern California, making the southland the state's twentieth-century stronghold of Protestant affiliation and ethos.

She also illustrates the importance of the "liberal" versus "conservative" division that overtook Protestantism in the twentieth century. Sister Aimee's religious roots and commitments were not to the oldline Protestant denominations that had striven for the religious custodianship of California in the nineteenth century, but to the Holiness-Pentecostal movement. Her entire ministry was based on commitment to key "conservative" or "evangelical" Protestant theological assumptions such as the divinely inspired revelatory nature of the Bible, the essential atonement accomplished for believers by the death of Jesus Christ, and the necessity of individual conversion to Christ for salvation. She joined other conservatives in rejecting theological accommodation to evolution theory and biblical criticism. As a Pentecostal, she went beyond assuming the supernatural character of salvation history and individual conversion to affirm the availability of supernatural power in the present, particularly through the gifts of the Spirit. McPherson and her followers are prime examples of the notable growth of various expressions of conservative or evangelical Protestantism in California since 1920.

Finally, Sister Aimee illustrates how Protestantism, wherever located on the continuum between liberal and conservative, also reflects the modifying influence of the social and cultural landscape of California. "Conservative" and "liberal," of course, are relative terms; therefore, being conservative does not preclude being innovative, nor does liberal preclude commitment to tradition. It might be noted then that it was McPherson's religious innovations more than her religious conservatism that brought her public attention. The Pentecostal movement was itself an innovation in American Protestantism. It extended the boundaries of traditional religious experience through emphasis on "baptism in the Spirit" accompanied by the sign of speaking in tongues and through the exercise of the gifts of healing and prophecy. In the priority Pentecostalism gave to the rule of the Spirit, it also was innovative in allowing women to take religious leadership, including pulpit preaching.

But in addition to reflecting these innovations in Protestant expression, McPherson intentionally appropriated the tools and ethos of modern media. With her use of radio, Sister Aimee was the first major figure in what scholars of American religion have termed "the electronic church." She used Hollywood props and staging in her religious services and offered herself in the style and appearance of a Hollywood "star." McPherson established herself in Los Angeles during the decade when Hollywood became the movie capital of the world.

Sister Aimee made Thompson Eade, a former vaudeville performer, her stage manager after his conversion at one of her meetings in 1924. As she settled down in her completed Angelus Temple, therefore, McPherson exchanged the unadorned appearance with which she had conducted her earlier itinerant tent meetings for dyed and bobbed hair and stylish dress. With Eade's expertise and McPherson's own dramatic gifts, she became known for her "Illustrated Sermons," in which she reinforced, with painted backdrops, rented props, and costumes, her simple sermon points. On one occasion, for example, she appeared in police uniform on a motorcycle, exclaiming "Stop in the name of the Lord!" Her 1926 disappearance from a California beach, and her reappearance a month later in Mexico with the explanation that she had been kidnapped, seemed to reinforce and even enhance her status as a religious celebrity. The flamboyance and optimism of her public image, coupled with the pain of her private life—she was married three times, and she died from an apparently accidental overdose of medication while conducting services in Oakland—were obvious symbols of the new power of the Hollywood ethos in American culture.

Sister Aimee therefore represented some important new developments in twentieth-century American Protestantism. California was not the only place manifesting these changes, but it was a place where such changes happened early and prominently. Sister Aimee, together with other representative people, movements, institutions, and events that will be described in what follows, do not mark California as religiously unique so much as they make California a distinctive reflector and bellwether of American religious developments.

California Protestantism Between the Wars

For many Americans, the 1920s and 1930s were rollercoaster years. The idealism of American participation in the Great War (1914-1918), capped by national prohibition and women's suffrage, was soon followed by highly publicized alienation from traditional perspectives among college-aged youth, artists, and writers. In the midst of general prosperity for the urban middle class, the tension between liberal and conservative Protestantism that had been building for years broke out into open theological warfare. The Presbyterian and Baptist denominations in particular became battlegrounds as militant, anti-modernist conservatives, dubbed "fundamentalists" in 1920, tried to rally other conservatives and moderates into coalitions that could establish and enforce biblicist guidelines within their respective denominations. Populist Democrat and evangelical Presbyterian William Jennings Bryan focused the anxiety of many conservatives on the potent issue of the teaching of evolution in the public schools. The trial of teacher John Scopes for violating a Tennessee anti-evolution law in 1925 was the highwater mark of militant Protestant conservatism's postwar attempt to exercise cultural authority. In this battle, conservatives were defeated, and their public ridicule led to the withdrawal and regrouping of many of the conservative militants into what came to be yet another major Protestant subculture—fundamentalism—adding to those already encountered: black, southern white, Asian, Hispanic, Holiness and Pentecostal subcultures.

Meanwhile, oldline Protestant denominations, largely identified as the churches of the white, native-born middle and upper classes, but by the 1920s with a membership that was more theologically diverse than ever, sought to move beyond religious conflict. Conservatives wanted to stress biblicist doctrine, conversionist experience, and evangelistic mission activism; but the moderate and liberal leadership of oldline Protestantism led their denominations toward organizational centralization, professionalization, and bureaucratization. These changes were accomplished by the muting of religious experience in favor of an emphasis on psychology, social ministry, and interdenominational cooperation.

Meanwhile, economic depression of the 1930s reinforced what has been called the "spiritual depression" that had set in upon the oldline denominations in the mid-1920s. The repeal of national prohibition in 1933 signaled the end of any remaining hopes for a "Christian America" in the image of Anglo-American Protestantism. This national experience of the oldline Protestant community amounted to what has been called a "second disestablishment" of religion in American history.

In California, the course of Protestantism between the wars generally reflected these developments, yet with significant regional variations. It also foreshadowed things to come.

Radio and the Churches

Aimee Semple McPherson was not the only Protestant in California to begin a significant radio ministry between the wars. Her rival for recognition as Los Angeles' most flamboyant Protestant was Robert "Fighting Bob" Shuler (1880-1965). In 1920 he assumed the pastorate at Trinity Methodist Church, a post he held until 1953. He was an outspoken conservative Southern Methodist who made no compromise with theological liberalism, and his preaching and publications fostered the growth of his congregation to over 5,000 members by the 1930s. A wealthy widow gave Shuler a radio station in 1926. Shuler quickly assumed a combative role in his calls over the air for "civic righteousness and for the extension of Christ's kingdom on earth." His broadcasts were called a significant factor in the election of a reform mayor of Los Angeles in 1929 and in the subsequent firing of the city's police chief (a few years earlier another city chief of police had been fired under Shuler's charges of drunkenness). Over the airwaves Shuler also attacked such individuals and institutions as publisher William Randolph Hearst, the public schools, the Chamber of Commerce, and the Roman Catholic Church. Protests by numerous citizens to the Federal Radio Commission (FRC) led to that agency's denial of the renewal of Shuler's broadcast license in 1931.

The radio ministry of Robert Shuler was brief and localized. Far more significant, and far more irenic, although no less theologically conservative, was the broadcasting begun by Charles E. Fuller (1887-1969). A native of Los Angeles, Fuller had attended Pomona College, married, and taken up a business career in Southern California before undergoing a conversion to fundamentalist evangelicalism in 1916. Supporting himself and his family with his business investments, he studied at the Bible Institute of Los Angeles (1919-1921) and built an independent fundamentalist congregation, Calvary Church, in Placentia between 1925 and 1933. Financial difficulties stemming from the Great Depression seem to have been at least one important factor in leading Fuller to consider trying something new in American Protestant broadcasting—a radio ministry independent of any formal church support or affiliation. In 1933 he left his congregation and bought Sunday time on a Long Beach radio station, paying for the programs with the contributions of listeners and the informal congregation who came to the services conducted live in the studio. In the next two years, Fuller perfected his broadcast style of unpretentious evangelistic Bible exposition combined with traditional hymn and gospel-song singing, naming his program "The Old Fashioned Revival Hour." After 1937, the program was distributed to over 450 radio stations in the United States, making the Los Angeles-based Fuller the first truly national radio minister.

Fuller, Shuler, and McPherson together illuminate the pioneering adaptation of modern media by conservative Protestants that took place in Southern California in the 1920s and 1930s. Northern California spawned no examples comparable in influence, perhaps because it was without the south's stimulus of the vibrant movie industry or the staggering migration of whites from the mid-section of the United States who were predisposed to support conservative ministries. Instead, a more liberal Protestantism dominated Northern California's religious institutions.

Even after radio and later television technology allowed for the dispersal of Protestant broadcasting, Southern California continued to be a major center. In 1947, for instance, Herbert W. Armstrong moved his Worldwide Church of God organization, founded ten years earlier, from Oregon to Pasadena. The move included his radio program. Armstrong's church, which included a college, a publishing arm, and eventually a television broadcast, spread nationwide a distinctive message of prophecy, Old Testament law and observances, and British Israelism (identifying Anglo-Saxons as the ten lost tribes of Israel).

The Beginning of Protestant "Southernization"

The relatively conservative social origins of many migrants to Southern California in the first half of the twentieth century is one factor helping to explain the strength of conservative Protestantism there. "Fighting Bob" Shuler typifies an important aspect of migration to the southland in the interwar period. Shuler had come to Los Angeles from a pastorate in Texas. In the 1920s some 250,000 white emigrants from the South Central states of Texas, Oklahoma, Missouri, and Arkansas moved to California, followed by another 300,000—derisively named "Okies"—in the 1930s. For the first time the South began to make a sizable contribution to California society, including Protestantism.

This migration made for a marked "southernization" of California Protestantism by 1940 in that the "Okie" population which settled in the southern portion of the Central Valley, especially in Kern County, altered the denominational mix in the state. They came from regions where the dominant Protestant groups were Southern Methodists and Southern Baptists, with smaller concentrations of Christian Churches (Disciples of Christ) and Churches of Christ and various holiness and pentecostal groups. In California, the Southern Methodists were too weak a presence and too preoccupied with a national merger with the Northern Methodists, consummated in 1939, to take advantage of the influx, and there was no Southern Baptist organization in the state in the 1920s and 1930s.

Protestant religion was too important to these ex-southerners, however, to languish for long. As did other immigrants before and since, they found forms of Protestantism that oriented them both to God and to the world around them. First to take advantage of the new immigrant pool were Holiness and Pentecostal groups. By the end of the 1930s, notes historian James N. Gregory, "nearly every town in the Central Valley boasted at least a Nazarene and Assemblies of God and often several other Pentecostal churches." The experiential emphasis and holiness moral code of these churches provided personal and communal meaning and dignity in a relatively familiar form for the socially marginal "Okies." As one adherent put it, "Sometimes I think I am worth nothing to the Lord or to anybody else, but when I realize what I am in His eyes, it makes me want to pray all the more."

Close behind the Holiness and Pentecostal groups were the Southern Baptists. The regional ties of the latter denomination kept it from expansion into California in the nineteenth century, and in 1912 it had formally agreed that the state was Northern Baptist territory. Southern Baptists who migrated to California, however, were not impressed by the Northern Baptist churches. One family, for example, tried the First Baptist Church of Shafter: "but then that didn't satisfy us Baptists from the South, from Oklahoma," they complained, "because it wasn't like we were used to." They and others in Shafter persuaded a Southern Baptist preacher from Arkansas to come in 1937. Other pastors arrived to minister to the newly arrived southerners. The San Joaquin Valley Missionary Baptist Association was organized in 1939, and in 1941 the fourteen churches of the association were officially accepted by the Southern Baptist Convention. Twelve years later, there were over 400 Southern Baptist congregations in California with a membership near 75,000.

Protestants and the Public Realm

The growth of radio ministries and the southernization of the Protestant community were not the only ways in which Protestants influenced the state of California during the 1920s and 1930s. The shock of liberal versus conservative Protestantism, like the shock of cultural disestablishment, experienced by oldline denominations in the urban northeast of the U.S. were somewhat muted in the experience of California's denominations because of their long-standing relative weakness in California society. Nonetheless, oldline Protestants in interwar California sought to maintain and, at times, even extend, their perspectives and institutions.

Take, for example, inter-denominational cooperation. Inter-Protestant ecumenism was not a new idea in 1920. The Protestant mission movement of the nineteenth century had begun interdenominationally, and Protestant revivalism and Sunday schools had enduring elements of nondenominational emphasis. All along the liberal-conservative Protestant continuum, cooperation continued alongside denominational independence. The organization of the Federal Council of the Churches of Christ in 1908 both reflected as well as spurred the creation of similar cooperative organizations at more local levels. For the oldline denominations, the dominant form of cooperation by 1920 was through local, state, and national church federations or councils.

The California State Church Federation came into being in 1913 as a result of the efforts of the San Francisco Church Federation—formed in 1906 in the wake of the great earthquake and fire—and similar organizations in Los Angeles and Sacramento. The stated purpose of the state federation was typical of such institutions in stressing "comity" (agreements among the denominations in where to plant new churches with a minimum of competition), and cooperation for "social betterment," which in 1913 included "the interests of the Sabbath" and "temperance" as well as "industry." The state federation offices were in Sacramento, and for much of the interwar period the leadership core was Methodist. The federation was particularly active in 1926. That year the federation worked with the National Park Service in establishing and maintaining an interdenominational church in Yosemite National Park.

Also in 1926, the organization attempted to rally the membership of its churches to vote on state measures having to do with race track gambling, prohibition enforcement, and Bible reading in the public schools. The federation's executive secretary blamed the defeat of the third measure on Northern California churches: "The churches were almost wholly united in the south, and greatly divided in the north." Tensions between the two halves of the state were eased somewhat with the reorganization of the federation in 1935. With a new name, the California Church Council, the federation provided separate executives for north and south. Separate executives, however, led to separate councils in 1943. California thus became the only state to have two councils. The federation movement belatedly came to recognize the importance of the long-standing social and cultural differences between the two parts of the state.

In the face of social and economic changes and religious diversity, Protestant political commitments became increasingly difficult to identify. For example, the brief rise of the Ku Klux Klan (KKK) in California between 1921 and 1926 had significant Protestant support. Yet Protestants also figured in opposition to the Klan. The KKK was originally a secret organization born in the wake of the defeat of the South in the Civil War, designed as a tool of political and racial intimidation of the enfranchised ex-slaves. In its early twentieth-century resurrection, the Klan again built on a southern base of white Protestant supremacy, yet with enough appeal in its anti-black, anti-Catholic, anti-Jewish, anti-immigrant message to attract many native-born whites in places outside the South. Such people were dislocated enough by urban society to respond to a group that on its face represented patriotic, Protestant "Americanism" and support for law and order in the face of "un-American" immigrants, radicals, and criminal violators of national prohibition.

In California, the KKK was strongest in the Central Valley and the southern portion of the state. The Reverend Shuler himself reportedly professed "to love the Klan for the enemies she has made," and Sister Aimee accepted $100 for a speech she made to the Oakland klavern in 1922. In Anaheim, the Klan was led by Leon L. Myers, pastor of the First Christian Church, and his men's Bible class formed the nucleus of the local klavern. The mayor and the majority of the city council elected in 1924 in Anaheim were Klansmen. Yet it was another Protestant pastor, Methodist James Allen Gerssinger, who helped rally opposition to the KKK, resulting in a decisive recall of the Klan-dominated city government in 1925.

California Protestantism, it is true, was still overwhelmingly composed of descendants of English and other northern Europeans. However, while some Protestants responded to "foreigners" with hatred, many others supported mission activity to help those "foreigners." Work among Chinese and Japanese settlers in California remained significant, particularly on the part of oldline denominations, in the period between the wars. The new activity, though, focused on Southern California's growing Mexican population. Immigration from Mexico increased greatly in the wake of the Mexican Revolution in 1910, and in the 1910s and 1920s oldline Protestant missions to Spanish-speaking peoples expanded. The Methodists of the Southern California Annual Conference organized a Spanish and Portuguese District in 1912 and a Spanish American Institute for industrial training in 1913. The Southern California Baptist Convention joined with the Los Angeles City Mission and the Northern Baptist Home Mission Society in 1932 to solidify earlier efforts to establish a theological school for Mexican-American Baptists in Los Angeles. The mission work of the oldline denominations was hampered by the mobility of the immigrants, however, and by their reluctance to accept the basic missionary goal of the assimilation of Spanish-speaking converts into Anglo culture.

In proportion to their resources, some Holiness and Pentecostal groups fared better among Mexicans than the oldline missions. By 1930, the Assemblies of God had three Spanish-speaking churches in Los Angeles and Orange Counties and a Latin American Bible Institute in San Diego. An intriguing example of Mexican Protestantism between the wars was the Apostolic Assembly of the Faith in Christ Jesus. This denomination grew out of the evangelism of

Mexican converts at the Azusa Street Apostolic Faith Mission in 1910. The group's founders followed Mexican migrants and preached a Pentecostal message with the distinctive addition that baptism was to be in the name of "Jesus only." "In the beginning," writes Manuel J. Gaxiola,

> the majority of the converts were workers in the fields, entire families of migrants who followed the harvest in California. They worked all day in the fields and at night they had a worship service that lasted four or five hours. They sang and preached with all the fervor and enthusiasm which only recently converted men can have. They composed their own hymns and sang them accompanied by the guitar and they spoke in tongues and prayed with all the strength of their lungs. [*La Serpienta y la Paloma* (1970), p. 163]

This fully Mexican-American denomination was formally organized in 1925, with some twenty congregations and perhaps 700 members, most residing in California. Despite tensions over practices of strong male leadership and required tithing and the pace of adaptation to Anglo-American society, by 1968 the denomination had eighty-eight California churches.

The Great Depression

The Great Depression put sudden and widespread economic constraints on California Protestants, as it did other religious groups. At the Pacific School of Religion in Berkeley, a drive for funds in 1932-1933 fizzled, faculty and staff had to take salary cuts, and seminary students found that few congregations had money to employ them as interns. The Southern California Baptist Convention had seen fifty-three new congregations established from 1923 to 1929. This growth was cut almost in half in the 1930s, the economic difficulties compounded by the disaffection of militant conservatives who transferred to other Baptist denominations. The 1932 (Northern) California Annual Conference of the Methodist Episcopal Church reduced the clergy's recommended salaries by one-third and established a Mutual Aid and Fellowship Fund, made up of voluntary contributions from conference members, to help clergy who had financial problems.

Protestants also ministered to the needs of Depression-era Californians. Aimee Semple McPherson's Angelus Temple Commissary was the most publicized of countless emergency aid programs run by churches. The "Okies," leaving behind the ravaged economy of the western South, found material as well as spiritual aid primarily from Holiness, Pentecostal, and Southern Baptist churches, but also from some oldline denomination pastors, including those working at government camps. Methodist Edgar E. Wilson of the California Division of Immigration and Housing assessed Okie needs in his *The Church and the Last American Migration*. Protestants divided, however, over the appropriateness of more radical responses to the Depression beyond private, voluntary aid. The Southern California Baptist Conference, for instance, sidestepped official comment in order to forestall controversy. The Methodist Southern California Annual Conference called for public ownership of utilities and the principal means of production and transportation, but other Methodists objected. The 1934 gubernatorial campaign of socialist Upton Sinclair, running as the Democratic candidate, "brought many tensions in congregations and in the Conference," recalled a Methodist of the California Conference. Sinclair lost, but the victory of New Dealer Democrat Culbert Olson in 1938 was due at least in part to many Protestant votes, including those of San Joaquin Valley "Okies."

The Second World War

In 1939 the San Francisco Bay Area staged the Golden Gate International Exposition. Business and community leaders of San Francisco desired to direct the nation's attention away from the upstart Los Angeles region. Despite significant labor unrest during the 1930s, San Francisco leaders wished to showcase two striking monuments to labor-business cooperation, accomplished with federal funding: the Bay Bridge (1936) and the Golden Gate Bridge (1937). Liberal Protestants, anxious to remind visitors to the fair that "our Democracy in America stands as one of the products of religion," spearheaded the creation of an interreligious committee for the purposes of constructing a Temple of Religion and Tower of Peace at the exposition. The funds were raised and the Temple and Tower, with exhibits, auditorium, and "Bible garden," were built on Treasure Island with the rest of the world's fair.

Over 10,000,000 people visited the Golden Gate International exposition. Yet, ironically, just as San Francisco's Panama-Pacific International Exposition of 1916 had been overshadowed by war, so was the 1939 fair. The Tower of Peace was mocked by events in Europe. The Temple of Religion seemed more a plea for recognition than an icon of self-assurance on the part of oldline Protestants in Northern California.

The Second World War affected California Protestantism in more ways than at the Golden Gate International Exposition. It ended the Depression, brought hundreds of thousands of new people to California, and exacerbated the racial prejudices of whites, thereby posing new challenges and fostering new developments for Protestantism in the Golden State.

Protestants and Japanese Internment

The Japanese surprise attack on Pearl Harbor in December 1941 awakened old racially-based fears of Asians among many Californians. Rumors of Hawaiian Japanese involvement in the Pearl Harbor attack made the presence of spies and saboteurs among the California Japanese seem an entirely reasonable suspicion. Only a few Protestants raised any protest over Executive Order 9066, issued in February 1942 by President Franklin Delano Roosevelt at the behest of Lt. Gen. John L. DeWitt, the commander of West Coast defenses. Under the provisions of the order, some 93,000 California Japanese, including tens of thousands of *nisei*, (second-generation Japanese born in the United States and therefore U.S. citizens) were forced to leave their homes and employment and, together with Japanese from the states of Oregon and Washington, placed in barbed-wire encircled "relocation centers" away from the coast.

Portions of California Protestantism, led by foreign and home missions leaders, had always sought, however ambiguously because of their conventional paternalism, to defend the Japanese residents in the state from white hostility. Such defense was too little and too late in early 1942. The president of the Church Federation of Los Angeles was "too busy" to testify on behalf of the Japanese when a U.S. House of Representatives' committee held hearings on evacuation in the city. The Church Council of Sacramento's words could sound hollow: "Japanese friends and fellow Americans, we believe in you. . . . God bless you and keep you." In general, though, once the initial hysteria had subsided, Protestants scrambled to soften the evacuation experience. Congregations, denominational organizations, and interdenominational institutions provided emergency aid as the Japanese were assembled for internment; some Protestants assumed powers of attorney for properties Japanese had to leave, while others visited the camps and tried to provide material and spiritual assistance to the internees. Protestant bodies began to urge hearing boards to determine the loyalty of individual internees, and churches were prominent sponsors when Japanese families returned in 1945.

Wartime Migration

While Japanese Californians were forced to leave the state because of the war, close to 3 million other Americans came to the state in the 1940s. Civilian immigrants came to fill defense-related jobs, particularly aircraft manufacture in the southland and shipbuilding in the north. Earlier "Okies" from the Central Valley were joined by some 620,000 new western Southerners, heading for the defense plants.

Among these migrants from the western South were over 125,000 black citizens. African-Americans moved into the formerly Japanese sections of Los Angeles and San Francisco and spilled over into other sections. Estimates of the black population of Los Angeles County jumped from slightly over 2.5 percent in 1940 to 4 percent in 1944. In the San Francisco Bay counties, the black population skyrocketed from an estimated 19,000 in 1940 to over 64,000 four years later.

California Protestants struggled to keep pace with the sudden inrush of people. Ministry to the armed forces and to the defense workers strained the resources of religious organizations only recently coping with Depression shortages.

Richmond, California, provides an illuminating, if extreme, case of Protestant responses to the war boom. In 1940, the industrial city on the northeast side of San Francisco Bay had a population of 23,600. With the decision of Henry J. Kaiser to locate his shipbuilding yards there, the city's population doubled, and doubled again; by 1947, the estimated number of people living in Richmond was over 100,000.

The old-line Protestant churches in the city studied the situation in 1947. They found the eleven churches that were members of the Richmond Council of Churches—four Northern Baptist, one Christian (Disciples of Christ), one Protestant Episcopal, two Methodist Episcopal, and three Presbyterian—had a total of some 4,000 members, or roughly 4 percent of the city's population. The council supervised another eleven temporary church programs among the war-housing areas. The future of these "community churches" was tenuous at best; a church survey by the Northern California-Western Nevada Council of Churches indicated that in the spring of 1945 the attendance at all East Bay United Church war-housing projects was slightly over 1,000. The Richmond church report described the council's projects as surviving only "by almost superhuman efforts." Apparently the liberal and middle class style and perspectives of the oldline churches had scant appeal to the newly arrived white and black laborers. Such a conclusion is reinforced by the existence of over thirty other churches in Richmond, including such conservative Protestant congregations as Full Gospel Assembly of God, Bethlehem Missionary Baptist, Faith Pentecostal Tabernacle, First Southern Baptist, Church of God in Richmond, Seventh-Day Adventist, Salvation Army, Church of God in Christ, Evangelical Free Church, and Church of the Nazarene. A similar report in 1945 by the Church Federation of Los Angeles revealed much the same picture: puzzlement and frustration of oldline Protestant churches in the face of immense opportunities and the growth of alternative traditions of Protestantism.

The Postwar Revival in California

Old-line Protestant discouragement in California would soon recede, for a time at least. In the decade and a half after the Second World War, American religion underwent a period of general growth that was significant enough for some to have characterized it as a "postwar revival." Judaism and Roman Catholicism experienced the boom along with the diverse segments of American Protestantism. California—"America only more so"—reflected the developments leading up to and constituting this resurgence.

Neo-orthodoxy, Neo-liberalism, and Neo-evangelicalism

American Protestantism's intellectual centers had begun in the East, and they remained east of the Mississippi River well into the twentieth century despite the presence of institutions of higher education in California since the 1850s. Before 1920, the existing colleges and seminaries were, as California society itself was, adolescent and provincial. Well before 1945, however, the increasing cultural authority exercised by California over the rest of the nation also began to be reflected in the realm of Protestant thought emanating from the Golden State. At the same time, major Protestant colleges and universities in California followed the general trend toward secular academic models.

The most important theological center of old-line Protestantism in California in the twentieth century continued to be in the greater San Francisco area, where the oldest schools of these denominations remained. There were two major exceptions to this Bay Area focus. First, conservative concern in Southern California over the suspected liberalization of the Berkeley Baptist Divinity School led to the founding of the California Baptist Theological Seminary in 1944. Residing at first in Los Angeles, in 1951 the school moved to Covina, where it remained until it was merged with the Berkeley seminary between 1968 and 1974. The second exception was the California seminary of the Methodists. A theological school had been affiliated with the University of Southern California since 1887. The cutting of the last formal Methodist ties to the university in 1952 prompted the Southern California Annual Conference to reorganize the school, which since 1957 has been located in Claremont.

By 1930, however, Berkeley was the site for the Episcopal seminary of the West Coast, the Northern Baptist seminary, the Congregationalist-rooted interdenominational Pacific School of Religion, and the Pacific Coast Unitarian seminary. The northern Presbyterian school remained across the Bay in San Anselmo, and Lutherans had moved a seminary to Berkeley by 1952.

Protestant liberal theological perspectives were most forcefully broadcast from the Pacific School of Religion. In general, the message of Protestant liberalism accented the immanence of God compared to traditional conceptions of divine transcendence; the use of historical criticism for understanding the Bible; and the importance of reinterpreting Christian thought in light of modern intellectual developments. Edwin T. Earl endowed an annual lecture series in 1901, and, until the 1940s, many prominent liberal Protestant luminaries delivered Earl lectures, including Lyman Abbott (1904), William Jewett Tucker (1906), Walter Rauschenbusch (1910), and Charles Clayton Morrison (1933). Among the school's faculty, John Wright Buckham, theologian at the school from 1903 to 1937, and William Frederick Bade, Old Testament professor from 1902 to 1936, published significant work in their respective fields.

In the 1930s, the influence of Swiss theologian Karl Barth and the writings of a new generation of old-line Protestant thinkers critical of aspects of the older liberalism led to altered theological perspectives. The new perspectives, termed "neo-orthodoxy" or "biblical theology," accented the transcendence of God and the intractability of sin, but it did so without rejecting historical criticism, modern thought, or social concern. The Earl lectures reflected the new trends with speakers such as Walter Marshall Horton (1940), Reinhold Niebuhr (1941), Emil Brunner (1955), and Paul Tillich (1963). Further, in the late 1930s and early 1940s John C. Bennett (theology) and James Muilenburg (Old Testament) helped make PSR a significant training school for neo-orthodoxy. Other faculty members who had national reputations by the 1950s included Jack Finegan (Old Testament) and Georgia Harkness (theology).

Conservative Protestant thought had always been present in the old-line Protestant denominations and seminaries of California in the nineteenth and early twentieth centuries. For example, militant conservatives had forced the resignation of Thomas Day, Old Testament professor at the Presbyterian seminary, in 1912, and they had brought about the collapse of the Berkeley Bible Seminary (Disciple of Christ) around the same time. But conservative Protestant energies during the early twentieth century had been directed more to developing institutional networks than to formal theological writing.

The 1940s, though, saw the beginnings of a new stage in conservatism. A new generation of conservatives who had not participated in the warfare of the 1910s and 1920s desired to reform fundamentalism in a way analogous to the neo-orthodox reformation of liberalism. This reformed fundamentalism, termed "neo-evangelicalism," desired to leave behind the anti-intellectual, culture-rejecting sectarianism of much of conservatism. Neo-evangelicals accented a thoughtful and more civil defense of traditional supernaturalism and an ecumenical yet conversionist mission outreach at home and abroad. The National Association of Evangelicals, begun in 1943, provided early and formal expression to this new development.

California became a major center of neo-evangelicalism with the founding of Fuller Theological Seminary in Pasadena in 1947. Charles Fuller's radio ministry provided the base of support for the new institution, and conservative Boston Congregationalist pastor Harold John Ockenga became the leader and assembled a faculty. At the opening convocation, Ockenga claimed California was the appropriate place for the school because "Here we have the recrudescence of a culture" and therefore the opportunity for the shaping presence of evangelical thought. During the early years, the leading luminaries were theologians Carl F.H. Henry, who left the school in 1956 to become the founding editor of the neo-evangelical magazine *Christianity Today*, and E.J. Carnell, a widely published scholar.

Protestant Youth, Christ for Greater Los Angeles, and the Garden Grove Community Church

In the late 1940s and the 1950s California Protestantism seemed to prosper. The state population grew to 10,500,000 in 1950 and to 15,700,000 in 1960, migration from within the United States making up a major portion of the increase. As veterans returned, married, and began families, and as the economic constraints of the Great Depression and war ended, white Americans in general and white Californians especially purchased new homes and cars and began to attend church as a family. A variety of Protestant expressions of the gospel found a more receptive audience in an atmosphere where the assumption of America's leadership of the "free world" seemed to require moral renewal and commitment.

The founding and growth of Fuller Seminary was one evidence of the "postwar revival" in California. Another evidence was the 1949 Los Angeles evangelism campaign of a young neo-evangelical, William F. "Billy" Graham (1918-). For eight weeks, Graham held forth in a mammoth tent able to hold several thousand. Media attention turned to him after a few celebrities, particularly "Okie" radio star Stuart Hamblin, were converted under Graham's simple preaching. The Hearst syndicate of newspapers, plus *Time*, *Newsweek*, *Life*, and other publications, talked about the "rising young evangelist." The Los Angeles meetings launched Graham on his way as the twentieth century's most famous and respected mass evangelist.

Preceding and paralleling Graham's success was a growing network of conservative Protestant youth ministries. Older organizations that had been geared to earlier generations of high school and college-aged youth, such as Christian Endeavor and the Student

Volunteer Movement, had atrophied as vital movements by 1940. Just as elements of conservative Protestantism, particularly in California, had been alert to the innovative possibilities of radio, however, so neo-evangelicals in the 1940s updated Protestant structures for youth. Youth for Christ rallies featured mass evangelistic programs presented in the idiom of the entertainment and youth cultures of the time. Graham had honed his public style as a featured speaker at Youth for Christ rallies in the 1940s. Another Youth for Christ evangelist, Robert W. Pierce, founded the California-based World Vision International, the largest neo-evangelical world relief agency, in 1950.

One college ministry, Campus Crusade for Christ, had important ties to the California context. William R. "Bill" Bright came to California from Oklahoma during the Second World War to begin a business career. He attended Hollywood Presbyterian Church, at first attracted by the monied people there but soon converted under the ministry of the congregation's director of Christian education, Henrietta C. Mears (1890-1963). Mears, a compelling Bible teacher, had made Hollywood Presbyterian a center for neo-evangelical youth work. During her career, she reportedly encouraged some five hundred young men to enter the ministry, primarily in the Presbyterian denomination, and she also founded an evangelical publishing house and the Forest Home conference center.

From Mears, Bill Bright picked up a vision for evangelism among college youth. He attended Fuller Seminary when it opened in 1947, but he left before finishing a degree in order to organize Campus Crusade for Christ in 1951. The new ministry quickly spread from the University of California at Los Angeles to other campuses across the country. Stressing evangelism through use of the booklet *Have You Heard of the Four Spiritual Laws?*, Campus Crusade is now international in scope and ministering beyond campuses. Its headquarters in San Bernardino oversees a staff of thousands and, in addition, a school of theology.

Billy Graham, World Vision, Henrietta Mears, and Campus Crusade, together with Fuller Seminary, typify the importance of Southern California in the growth of neo-evangelicalism after the Second World War. Related but distinct developments took place surrounding the ministry of Robert H. Schuller (1926-). The young Schuller arrived in Garden Grove in 1955, sent by the Reformed Church in America—a small old-line Protestant denomination of

Dutch heritage—to start a new congregation. Schuller's task was representative of much of California Protestantism in the 1950s, a time of church building among the growing suburbs of middle-class California.

Schuller's assignment may have been unremarkable, but his fulfilling of it was extraordinary. Convinced that reaching the unchurched demanded unconventional approaches, he appealed to the car culture of Orange County by renting a drive-in theater and preaching to the automobile-encased audience from the top of the snack bar. A conventional church building was soon constructed, but the drive-in services were continued. Schuller drew people to his church by deemphasizing his old-line denominational ties, emphasizing instead a "positive thinking" that flourished nationally in mid-twentieth-century American Protestantism, led by the popular preacher and writer, Norman Vincent Peale, minister of New York City's Marble Collegiate Church. Schuller sought to address what he identified as the primary need of his middle-class suburban audiences: self-esteem. In Schuller's retranslation of the gospel, Jesus Christ bore our loss of self-esteem in his death on the cross so that when we turn to Christ in faith, we have the basis for self-worth and a consequent life of "possibility thinking."

Schuller became his own best example of possibility thinking. In 1961 he dedicated a new church building that combined conventional seating and massive doors that opened to the parking lot outside—a walk-in/drive-in church. He added a Tower of Hope in 1968, housing offices and counseling services, and standing high enough, crowned by a ninety-foot high lighted cross, to be visible for miles. An organization for disseminating Schuller's principles of church growth was begun in 1969. The following year, the "Hour of Power" appeared on television. Currently, it is one of the most widely-watched religious programs in America. The architectural capstone to Schuller's ministry was completed in 1980: the $20 million Crystal Cathedral, extending the walk-in/drive-in concept in size and in physical linkage to the Southern California climate.

Rejecting criticisms that he replaced traditional Christian understandings of sin and redemption with a gospel of material success, Schuller stressed that he merely retranslated the gospel in order to reach "the affluent non-religious American." This was a different audience from those who gravitated to Aimee Semple

McPherson's Foursquare Gospel preaching a half-century earlier. Yet like Sister Aimee, Robert Schuller successfully utilized Hollywood-style mass media to bring millions of Americans in touch with Protestant Christianity.

Moreover, if Schuller and his programs distinctively reflected the exaggerated twentieth-century suburban society of Los Angeles and Orange counties, they also represented only one of several emerging trends of Protestantism in California as we move past the decade of the 1950s into current times.

Suggested Further Reading:

Carter, Paul. *The Decline and Revival of the Social Gospel: Social and Political Liberalism in American Protestant Churches, 1920-1940*. Ithaca, N.Y.: Cornell University Press, 1954.

Cavert, Samuel McCrea. *Church Cooperation and Unity in America, A Historical Review: 1900-1970*. New York: Association Press, 1970.

Ernst, Eldon G. *Moment of Truth For Protestant America: Interchurch Campaigns Following World War One*. Missoula, Mont.: Scholars' Press, 1974.

Gregory, James N. *American Exodus: The Dust Bowl Migrations and Okie Culture in California*. New York: Oxford University Press, 1989.

Herberg, Will. *Protestant, Catholic, Jew: An Essay in American Religious Sociology*. Garden City, N.Y.: Doubleday, 1955.

Hogue, Harland E. *Christian Seed in Western Soil: Pacific School of Religion Through a Century*. Berkeley: Pacific School of Religion, 1965.

Holland, Clifton L. *The Religious Dimension in Hispanic Los Angeles: A Protestant Case Study*. South Pasadena: William Carey Library, 1974.

Hutchison, William R., editor. *Between the Times: The Travail of the Protestant Establishment in America, 1900-1960*. Cambridge: Cambridge University Press, 1989.

Lothrop, Gloria Ricci. "West of Eden: Pioneer media evangelist Aimee Semple McPherson in Los Angeles." *Journal of the West* 27 (1988).

Marsden, George. *Reforming Fundamentalism: Fuller Seminary and the New Evangelism*. Grand Rapids, Mich.: Eerdmans, 1987.

Marty, Martin E. *Second Chance for American Protestantism*. New York: Harper & Row, 1963.

Meyer, Donald B. *The Protestant Search for Political Realism, 1919-1941*. Berkeley: University of California Press, 1961.

Miller, Robert M. *American Protestantism and Social Issues, 1919-1939*. Chapel Hill: University of North Carolina Press, 1958.

Nash, Gerald D. *The American West Transformed: The Impact of the Second World War*. Bloomington, Ind.: Indiana University Press, 1985.

6 The Pilgrimage in Upheaval: Restructuring California Protestantism Since 1960

In 1958, nearly four centuries after England's Sir Francis Drake and company initiated the Protestant religious presence in California, James A. Pike became the Protestant Episcopal Church Bishop of California. For the next eight years (1958-1966) this "self-governing American branch of the Anglican Communion" centered much of its attention on the colorful and controversial California bishop. With frequent national exposure, Bishop Pike became something of an archetype of the upheavals within American Protestantism during the decade of the 1960s, especially as this turmoil engaged California.

Born in Oklahoma, James A. Pike (1913-1969) had grown up in California, graduating from Hollywood High School and the University of California at Los Angeles. Raised in the Roman Catholic Church, he rejected Catholicism during his college years. He then took law degrees at UCLA and at Yale, practiced law in Washington, D.C. (1938-42), and became a U.S. Naval officer during World War II. Meanwhile, he had become drawn to the Protestant Episcopal Church, and after the war he became an ordained priest in 1946, studying at Union Theological Seminary in New York City. As chaplain at Columbia University (1949-52) and dean of St. John the Divine Cathedral in New York (1952-58) he became a popular public preacher, writer, and television religious personality (the "Dean Pike Show"). He had presented fairly conventional mainline

Protestant doctrine, within the catholic-oriented Anglican Episcopal tradition, prior to his return to California in 1958.

By 1958, however, Pike's theological perspective was changing, in tune with the time and forecasting the decade ahead. The civil rights movement, led by black Baptist minister Martin Luther King, Jr., had made its first challenge to institutionalized racism in the South, dramatically affecting Protestant church life and theology. Soon Protestants nationwide would feel the divisive and dislocating impact of radical social, intellectual, and religious departures from established patterns. Bishop Pike, from his San Francisco-based diocese, would become caught up in all of these "counter-cultural" forces of the 1960s.

In California, Pike came to the fore as a popular example of liberal Protestant social and theological reformism. He challenged theological tradition, for example, by openly suggesting that several points in the historical creeds of Christianity (such as the virgin birth of Jesus) should not be interpreted literally. From within his own denomination he was accused of heresy in 1961, 1965, and 1966, and only his skill as a lawyer and the desire of many Episcopalians to keep the lid on unseemly controversy averted a church trial.

If many Protestants felt uncomfortable with Bishop Pike's theological assertions, he in turn became uncomfortable by clergy and laity being caught up in the surging tongue-speaking movement among Episcopal and other churches. In a pastoral letter of 1963 he warned the diocese of the "heresy in embryo" of this charismatic movement.

At the same time, Bishop Pike used his church position to further his increasingly radical social views and actions. He served as chair of the California Advisory Committee on Civil Rights. In the battle to defend the state's Rumford Fair Housing Act of 1963, Pike was characteristically outspoken. "It is my duty as your Bishop," he wrote in one of his pastoral letters, "to urge you to present yourself at the polls, not only to vote for the candidates of your conscientious choice, but also to cast your NO vote on Proposition 14" (which challenged the legality of the Fair Housing Act). Pike also supported grape pickers' strikes, civil rights marches, ordination of women, and urged more humane treatment of alcoholics and homosexual persons.

Personal tragedy further complicated the last few years of Pike's life. His son's suicide plus the breakup of his marriage seemed to be the catalyst for bringing to a head Pike's disillusionment with the institutional church. He became fascinated with psychic phenomena in hopes of making contact with his dead son. In 1966 he resigned his position as bishop, preaching his farewell sermon to over 2,500 persons at Grace Cathedral. Described in 1967 as "a celebrity cleric . . . only one cut below Pope Paul and Billy Graham," he broke all ties with the church two years later when his request that his remarriage be blessed was publicly refused by his successor, Bishop Kilmer Meyers. But he remained committed to Jesus. His life ended when his car broke down in the Judean wilderness, where he had traveled to research the origins of Christianity.

The California experiences of Bishop James A. Pike touched on several areas that would help define the American Protestant pilgrimage during the later decades of the twentieth century. In California, as in the nation overall, this pilgrimage featured movements of civil rights and liberation, of youth-centered counterculture and "new ageism," of continuing liberal-conservative division, and of increasing diversity within the overall Protestant community.

Civil Rights and Liberation Movements

Prior to the 1960s American Protestantism, despite its internal conflict and divisions, remained solidly identified with the mainline of national cultural identity and public social institutions and ideology. This national prestige somewhat enhanced the Protestant impact on California public life, despite its historic minority religious position. During the 1960s, however, the counter-cultural forces in American life associated with civil rights and liberation movements, plus the anti-war movement during the Vietnam war years, broke apart any remnants of a mainline Protestant hegemony. That hegemony had been founded primarily on white Anglo-European church traditions, with predominantly white male leadership. In California, as in the nation generally, these traditions met unprecedented resistance from within. Issues focused on race and ethnicity, gender, and sexual orientation.

Civil Rights and Black Power

Black Protestant churches in California, as in other regions of the nation, had been at the heart of African American community life since before the Civil War. Though the Civil War ended slavery in the Old South, race prejudice and discrimination bound black African Americans together as an oppressed people. To varying degrees as conditions allowed, black churches became spiritual and social centers, even the locus of political power, in African American communities. Their theology of deliverance from oppression permeated preaching and singing, and their authority within the black communities was brought to bear on specific issues. In late-nineteenth-century California, for example, black clergy had helped make their churches the foci of political organizing for such black civil rights as the right to vote, to receive public education, and to enjoy full equality in courts of law.

Black Americans' civil rights, however, came slowly. By the start of the twentieth century little real progress had been made. Indeed, segregation and discrimination of black people received official sanction by actions of Congress and the Supreme Court. Second-class citizenship had become part of "the American Way," and segregation was nowhere more visible than in the life of the churches. In 1909 the National Association for the Advancement of Colored People (NAACP) was formed to advocate the rights of black citizens in courts of law, with strong black church support. Slowly, black Americans gained some representation in government and industry during the 1920-40s, though discrimination persisted—even in the armed forces during World War II. In 1949 President Truman integrated the armed forces and federal service, thereby signifying a new stage in the struggle of black Americans for social justice with focus on integration and equal opportunity.

In 1954 the Supreme Court decision (*Brown* v. *Board of Education of Topeka*) that "separate educational facilities are inherently unequal" marked the beginning of the nation's reluctant coming to terms with the issues of segregation and racism. The modern civil rights movement began the next year with the 1955-56 Montgomery bus boycott by black citizens, catapulting the young Baptist minister, Martin Luther King, Jr., into the role of the movement's primary leader and spokesperson.

The emergence of the modern civil rights movement, energized greatly by the black churches, happened during the years of enormous increase in California's African American population. Religious surveys during the mid-1940s indicated that the state's black population experienced a far greater growth rate during World

War II than the overall population. This growth continued. Between 1950 and 1970 the number of black Californians rose from 460,000 (nearly 4.5 percent of the population) to 1.4 million (7 percent of all Californians). Throughout these years black churches increased in number and size, and the civil rights movement took hold in the state.

In 1948 black Berkeley pharmacist W. Byron Rumford was elected to the State Assembly where, with Democratic party support, he formulated several measures enhancing equal justice. The culmination of this legal reform was the Rumford Fair Housing Act, passed by the legislature in 1963. The California Real Estate Association challenged the Rumford law, however, with Proposition 14 the following year. The major Protestant denominations, predominantly white, generally joined black Californians in opposing the initiative, but the proposition passed.

Proposition 14 was eventually overturned when the United States Supreme Court upheld the ruling of the California Supreme Court that the measure was unconstitutional. But meanwhile black outrage, together with a new black and white social radicalism, gelled in the state. Rioting in Watts, the black ghetto of Los Angeles, in the summer of 1965 resulted in thirty-four people killed, over one thousand injured, and forty million dollars in property damage. The following year, the Black Panther party was founded in Oakland. This new organization, with some connecting links to church parishes, drew on revolutionary socialism to shape a program of black pride and militancy—"black power." Among black radicals, Angela Davis gained special attention, first because of the denial of her reappointment to the faculty of the University of California at Los Angeles due to her political views, later because of her trial (and eventual acquittal) for complicity in a violent escape attempt by black prison inmates in Marin County. The oldline United Presbyterian denomination experienced internal tumult when a denominational agency gave $10,000 to Davis's defense fund in 1971.

The movement for civil rights and radical expressions of black power found nourishment from, and affected the life of, black Protestant churches in California as in the nation generally. By the end of the 1960s, black church leaders, theologians, historians and social scientists were giving fresh analysis and expression to the African American religious heritage and contemporary experience.

Books on black theology articulated the black churches' historic emphasis on themes of liberation and hope. Such organizations as the National Conference of Black Churchmen and the Alamo Black Clergy (a San Francisco-Oakland Bay Area caucus) provided networks of mutual support and identity to black church leaders within both the old-line, predominantly white denominations and the black Baptist and Methodist denominations. Local churches' programs of social mission and evangelism were rejuvenated.

Though manifested in great variety (a characteristic of Protestantism generally) the black church experience is well-exemplified in Oakland's Allen Temple Baptist Church. Organized in 1919 as a Northern (now American) Baptist mission with twenty-one members, Allen Temple eventually became aligned also with the black Progressive National Baptist Convention. Led by Pastor J. Alfred Smith, Sr., the church has grown to over 4,000 members drawn from a broad cross-section of Oakland's African American Community. Its 1,200-seat sanctuary normally is filled, with 300-400 overflow seating in a fellowship hall, for two Sunday morning worship services, one being broadcast over station KDIA radio. Powerful preaching that artistically integrates personal and social themes in rhythmic form, surrounded by music from several choirs, evokes vocal congregational responses. Out of this central worship experience have developed elaborate programs of ministries to family life and to many special interest groups of all ages. Among community outreach ministries are educational programs; food, clothing, shelter, and employment programs; a multi-faceted athletic program; a prison ministry and re-entry program; a health services program and a community drug crisis program; a senior citizens and handicapped persons housing complex; and a public ministries committee promoting economic and social justice in the community-at-large. "It is hard to think of any community action that hasn't been impacted by Allen Temple," noted Oakland's mayor Lionel Wilson in 1985. "We can't just be concerned about the sweet by and by," explained Pastor Smith. "We need to be concerned about the nasty here and now."

Other Liberation Movements

By the end of the 1960s other groups of California Protestants had begun likewise to assert their liberation from oppressive conditions they experienced. Asian Pacific Americans, Hispanic Americans, women, and gay and lesbian persons especially began to challenge the status quo and assert their claims to justice and distinctive identities. All have been Protestant expressions of, and involvements in, movements within society-at-large.

Previous chapters noted the distinctive presence of Asian and Pacific American Protestants in California since mid-nineteenth century. The 1960s witnessed a new thrust of racial-ethnic cultural self-consciousness especially among Chinese and Japanese churches. Asian caucuses were formed within the larger denominations to advocate greater recognition of Asian cultural expressions and Asian representation in ecclesiastical power structures. Renewed emphasis on liberation from racist socio-economic discrimination also defined the Asian churches' agenda. As the Asian Pacific presence in California continues to increase and diversify dramatically with the new immigrants from Southeast Asia, the older Asian Pacific American churches themselves experience challenges to traditional boundaries of their cultural religious expressions. Protestants among the more recent immigrants, for example, often are far more conservative theologically, as well as more Asian in cultural orientation, than are the older Asian American churches. Religious social activism, moreover, can be divisive within the Asian American community as a whole.

Equally challenging to old established traditions are the rapidly proliferating Hispanic Protestant churches. During the 1960s, buoyed by the black civil rights movement, César Chavez and the United Farm Workers Movement began successfully to organize for social justice. The resulting labor strikes and grape boycotts brought mixed responses from Protestant churches, ranging from radical support to extreme opposition. The migrant workers' movement, however, not only pricked the social conscience of old-line Anglo churches; it also helped raise the consciousness of Hispanic people, both citizens and migrants, of the value of their distinctive cultural-religious heritage in their struggle for social-economic liberation. It was out of the Latin American churches, both Catholic and Protestant, that a "theology of liberation" (God's fundamental commitment to liberating the poor and oppressed) was born. Yet even more dramatic has been the rapid spread of evangelical pentecostalism among Hispanic people, especially the more recent immigrants. In recent years the massive influx of new arrivals from Latin America, including legal and "undocumented" refugees from war-torn countries, has further challenged the churches' social mission orientations and priorities. The decision by some churches to offer sanctuary to "undocumented" refugees has divided Protestants as well as other Californians.

The 1960s also produced the modern movement for women's liberation, building upon earlier women's rights movements, but now with larger goals, including goals within the churches. Protestant women had struggled for their social and religious rights since the early years of California statehood. Women's mission societies had provided opportunity for religious leadership, and church-related women had given strong support for women's civil rights, such as suffrage. A handful of twentieth-century Protestant women had become prominent religious leaders, such as Sister Aimee in Los Angeles during the 1920s and Dr. Bebe Patten who became evangelist and dean of the Oakland Bible Institute during the late 1940s. But these women had broken through traditional barriers, reflected in comments by one of Bebe's students in the school's 1946 publication, *The Portal*:

> I, being a woman, am doubly grateful for the chance that I have had to preach here at the Oakland Bible Church, realizing the prejudice there is in Christendom today against women doing anything. But if God be for us, who can be against us?

In fact, many were against women asserting themselves within the churches. Overall, the denominational traditions had preserved a largely patriarchal religion that portrayed a masculine God ("the Father") and taught the submission of women to men. Very few women, prior to 1960, had even attempted to become ordained clergy. Normally women did not preach, did not hold offices of church leadership, did not study theology much less write it or teach it. Georgia Harkness, a Methodist Church leader and Professor of Applied Theology at Berkeley's Pacific School of Religion during the 1950s, was a notable exception.

By the decade of the 1970s women's consciousness (and some men's) had been raised to a new level. Christian feminists were challenging every restrictive and "sexist" aspect of church life and thought. They called for gender-inclusive language in worship and in theological texts. They enrolled in seminaries to prepare for church leadership, including ordination. Through denominational agencies and interdenominational organizations such as Church

Women United they advocated women's social, political, economic, and religious equality.

The Christian feminist movement has had far-reaching impact on California Protestantism, as in Protestantism nationwide. The major seminaries now teach curricula influenced by women's concerns to classes often comprised of as many women as men. Women are being ordained, though they still find it difficult to find church ministerial employment. It was a significant event, therefore, when Leontine Kelly, a black woman, in 1984 was appointed bishop of the United Methodist Church, California-Nevada Conference.

More recent, and more controversial within the churches, has been the movement for gay and lesbian rights. Opposition to sexual orientation other than heterosexuality, especially if sexuality is practiced, is deeply rooted in Christian tradition. With increasing numbers of persons declaring openly their gay and lesbian sexual orientation, debates have raged within the churches over whether this sexuality is natural or unnatural, a sickness or sin to be cured or condemned, thus an acceptable life-style or not. Most denominations have rejected ordination for openly gay or lesbian candidates, while some congregations have openly welcomed persons of diverse sexual orientations and life-styles into their membership. In 1968 Troy Perry, a Pentecostal minister, founded the Metropolitan Community Church in Los Angeles. Out of this church emerged the Universal Fellowship of Metropolitan Community Churches, with congregations nationwide. Homosexuals always have been among Protestant church membership, of course, but the coming "out of the closet" of persons declaring and living these sexual orientations within church life marks a major departure from traditional Protestant social mores. Advocacy of gay and lesbian rights, moreover, can be fully understood only within the historical context of the larger civil rights and counter-culture movements of the 1960s, a topic to which we now turn.

Youth Rebellion, Radical Religion, and New Age

The civil rights movement proved to be a model and a training ground for the college generation of the 1960s. Many of these "baby boomers" (those constituting a numerical bulge in America's post-World War II population) loudly rejected the social and political values of their parents' generation. Racial injustice and the United States' involvement in the Vietnam War during the later 1960s contradicted professed American idealism in the view of many white young people—especially those of middle and upper socio-economic class. Rock music, marijuana, and psychedelic drugs lay ready to be appropriated for a self-conscious youth revolt.

The New Left and Radical Religion

The youth revolt took two overlapping but distinct directions. Each found prototypical expression in California. The first direction was overtly political. The catalytic event for the "New Left" took place at the University of California at Berkeley in the fall of 1964. The attempt to enforce university regulations prohibiting the solicitation of funds for social and political activities led to what became known as the Berkeley Free Speech Movement. Hundreds of students began to apply tactics of civil disobedience—tactics borrowed from the civil rights movement—to pressure the university to allow "free speech." Campus unrest spread across the country, but Berkeley remained a center of radical protest against racism, the Vietnam War, and the capitalist "establishment." In 1969 one person was killed in rioting over the university's attempt to reclaim "People's Park"—a Berkeley landmark of social protest.

The second direction of youth revolt was more cultural. Berkeley and the Haight-Ashbury district of San Francisco became the focus of a "counterculture" of "hippies." Those "flower children" who were "hip" stressed the rejection of conventional white middle-class values and "tuned in" to rock music, drug use, casual recreational sex, and (for some) communal living. The 1967 "Summer of Love" in Haight-Ashbury and the 1969 Altamont Festival of rock music were two seminal events in this counterculture movement as expressed in California.

Studies of contemporary American religious history suggest that the baby boom generation tended to leave the churches, particularly old-line Protestant denominations, when they reached college age. This helps explain the nationwide downturn in old-line Protestant church membership that began in the mid-1960s, coincident with the youth revolt. The denominational leadership of the old-line groups tended to share many of this generation's sentiments, stressing social criticism and social activism. Indeed, many liberally-inclined Protestant members supported this activist trend. But many others, often theologically and socially more conservative, objected. Neither response, however, captured the imagination of the counter-culture generation under age thirty, and church involvement diminished as an avenue for activist youth.

The youth revolt did not mean, however, that a generation of young people disappeared from Protestantism. The evangelical youth ministries were well-placed to reach many high school and college students in the 1960s and later decades. Moreover, the more liberal churches found ways to maintain points of contact with political protest movements. In several directions the youth generation introduced radical new expressions of California Protestantism.

The Berkeley Free Church exemplified "New Left" Protestantism. This church came into being out of a 1967 mission effort by old-line churches in the campus area. Richard York, an Episcopal seminary student who held the Free Church together, provides a vivid and illuminating description of traditional Christian symbols and rites within the radical leftist context:

> This week about eight of us were there. . . . We went around the circle . . . criticizing ourselves for chauvinism, counter-revolutionary attitudes, sloth, not being upfront, oppressing someone. When we were done, someone read from Luke and Matthew about Jesus washing feet to give us an example of his way of serving the people instead of exploiting them. Then we passed around a basin of water and all washed our hands . . . for dinner.
>
> Halfway through dinner the bread was broken and we were reminded that Jesus did this with his collective and that to eat it here has special meaning: it is like signing a revolutionary manifesto, like joining the Movement again. . . . Eating it lightly, you condemn yourself to your own ego-tripping or elitism, because you betray the collective body. . . . Then the wine was poured—"this is the Constitution of the New Society in my Blood." After dinner we poured more wine and drank toasts, responding to each with the amen of "Right on." . . . Late in the night, the age-old revolutionary meal over, we went home. [Quoted in M.B. Bloy, Jr., *Search for the Sacred* (1972), pp. 87-88]

Reflecting the loose structure of much of the "New Left," this church effectively died in 1972, but much of its ethos continued for several years in the magazine *Radical Religion*.

The Jesus Movement

Much of "New Left" Protestantism melded into liberation theologies. More significant in terms of numbers of youth affected, was the Jesus movement. Portions of the youth counterculture of the late 1960s and early 1970s showed signs of fascination with Jesus as a countercultural figure. While the Berkeley Free Church interpreted Jesus in an explicitly political way, many more groups came to more traditional interpretations.

One example is the Christian World Liberation Front (CWLF). This group began in 1969 under the auspices of Campus Crusade, but the decision by Jack Sparks and his co-workers to adapt the countercultural lifestyle in order to gain a hearing in the Berkeley campus culture led to the independence of the new ministry. Jesus was presented as "the alternative," both to the establishment and to the New Left. The new group made their presence known on campus, particularly through innovative leaflets and posters. The second issue of CWLF's newspaper, *Right On*, depicted Jesus in a wanted poster as a "Notorious Leader of a worldwide liberation movement" who is extremely dangerous because "He changes men and sets them free" and because he is "rumored to have no regard for conventional dress standards" and "hangs around slum areas." Christian houses—"a cross between Christian dormitory and commune"—were established for staff and converts, and a ranch and a street-theater group were maintained for a time. CWLF represented the reappearance of Protestant primitivism—a reappropriation of the "first times" of New Testament experience and community—refracted through countercultural informality and spontaneity. Moreover, CWLF retained a distinct sympathy for radical cultural and political criticism. This "New Left" evangelicalism, or "young evangelicalism," survived the passing of CWLF. It has informed such Berkeley institutions as New College (a graduate school for Christian laypeople that was an outgrowth of the Crucible, a Christian "free university") and *Radix*, the successor to *Right On*.

The Charismatic Movement

Another expression of the Jesus movement was reflected in the growing importance of the Charismatic movement that emerged in the 1960s, perhaps most visibly in California. Just as neo-evangelicalism represented a new generation of fundamentalists, the

Charismatic movement represented a new generation of pente-costalism. Demos Shakarian, a California millionaire dairy farmer, had founded the Full Gospel Business Men's Fellowship International (FGBMFI) in Los Angeles in 1951. Through prayer breakfasts and conventions, the group sought to smooth the rough edges of Pentecostalism and carry it to the non-Pentecostal business realm. The work of FGBMFI and others encouraged the appropriation of healing signs and wonders—"Spirit-baptized" Christianity—without affiliation with the traditional Pentecostal denominations. The movement began to spread widely and permeate even some old line churches. In some situations this caused tensions.

In 1960 Dennis Bennett, rector of St. Mark's Episcopal Church in Van Nuys, announced to his congregation his experience of baptism in the Holy Spirit. Soon thereafter he resigned his post in the face of disapproval both from within the congregation and from his bishop. National media attention to the incident helped focus among Charismatic converts a sense of calling to the renewal of non-Pentecostal Protestantism. By 1975 the Charismatic movement had spread its influence throughout old-line Protestant denominations. It also had made impact on its parent, traditional Pentecostalism. Melodyland Christian Center in Anaheim, for example, which, following the purchase of the Melodyland Theater complex in 1969, came to include a delinquency prevention center, a high school, a college, and a school of theology, grew in part because of Assembly of God pastor Ralph Wilkerson's emphasis on charismatic ecumenicity.

The Charismatic movement's stress on renewal of Christianity through experience of the Spirit, exercise of spiritual gifts, and informal style of worship proved appealing to many young people "turned off" by more conventional middle-class churches. Charles "Chuck" Smith began a distinctive ministry to hippies and drug addicts in the Costa Mesa area in the late 1960s. His approach included Christian rock concerts, mass baptisms in the surf at Corona del Mar, and Christian communes combined with more traditional religious services. The Chapel has grown to an immense community of perhaps 35,000 people within a network of "Calvary Chapels," and it also has spawned Vineyard Christian Fellowship. The latter, under the leadership of John Wimber, formerly a pastor of the Calvary Chapel in Yorba Linda, separated from Calvary Chapel largely because of Wimber's more overt emphasis on "signs and wonders" in the life of the church. Calvary Chapel has exhibited little of the socially critical edge of CWLF. In a sense, therefore, CWLF and its legacy compared with Calvary Chapel Ministries illustrates enduring differences in the cultural ethos of Northern and Southern California. Another part of Calvary Chapel's significance resides in its lineage. Chuck Smith received his theological training at LIFE Bible College—Aimee Semple McPherson's school. Calvary Chapel is thus a continuation of the adaptive, innovative approach of Sister Aimee in both reflecting and shaping twentieth-century Southern California life. The CWLF, by contrast, grew out of politicized, activist Northern California life.

New Age

The greatest challenge to modern California Protestantism's ability to adapt and innovate religiously within the counter-cultural movement of the past quarter century without losing its essential identity, however, has come with the flourishing of what in the 1980s became known as the New Age movement. New Age refers to a great variety of spiritual interests, experiences, and commitments with direct connections to the 1960s rebellions but also with much earlier roots. New Age "aquarian religion" looks throughout religious history for spiritual insights and nourishment, and it thus is essentially syncristic. In popular bookstores nationwide, sections labeled New Age, usually alongside or in place of sections labeled Religion or Christianity, produce enormous sales. Book titles refer to Greek and Roman mythology, eastern Hindu and Buddhist mysticism and reincarnation, dream analysis and psychic phenomena, occultism and astronomy, and Native American tribal nature-spirituality.

Throughout the history of western civilization these kinds of popular spiritual orientations, unbound by Christian dogma, have surrounded and penetrated the churches. American Protestantism has always engaged popular movements of naturalism and supernaturalism. Since mid-nineteenth century, however, the California environment has been especially conducive to spiritual innovations and thus the flourishing of new religious movements alongside the established world religions. What distinguished the 1960s was the massive outpouring of spiritual expressions, mostly among the younger generation—a new religious consciousness explicitly counter to anything resembling conventional American Christianity, and usually linked to social-political protest. During the 1970s the new religiosity gradually lost much of its political identity, some of it redirected inward into the "human potential movement" of encounter groups, primal therapy, biofeedback, transcendental meditation, and humanistic psychology. Then, as the boomer generation matured during the 1980s, the once counter-cultural spirituality became an established popular ingredient in California's diverse social environment.

New Age spirituality thus transcends Protestant identity even as it challenges that identity. Overall it proclaims liberation from all religious orthodoxies, though it usually is tolerant of traditional Christian and other world religious teachings and practices. Most scholars recognize in the New Age movement a profound spiritual yearning among persons who have found little satisfaction within conventional churches. Frequently church leaders criticize New Ageism as modern pagan challenges to Christian faith, while the most conservative Protestants often condemn the movement as "satanic heresy." Yet New Age orientations are penetrating both liberal and conservative churches as some of their members seek new spiritual meaning and vitality within the community frameworks of conventional Christian traditions.

In April of 1990 the *San Francisco Chronicle* reported on a "Business of God" luncheon meeting in the Bankers Club in the city's Bank of America skyscraper. Pollster George Gallup, Jr. had spoken about "the pervasiveness of New Age thinking in this part of the country." Gallup, an evangelical Episcopalian, concluded that New Age and Christianity "cannot possibly exist side-by-side." Yet a *Chronicle* poll indicated that in Northern California, at least, they do live side-by-side and often "in the souls of individual believers"— perhaps 25 percent of Protestant and Catholic Christians. If so, then California Protestantism has added yet another major ingredient to its historic variety of expressions.

California Protestant Identities

"Churches opt for pleasant names to downplay theological identities." So read a *Los Angeles Times* article in December 1990. The movement to camouflage denominational identity is spreading around the nation, primarily, it seems, from Southern California. Newer evangelistic-oriented churches especially are trying to attract members from among the unchurched majority of California's population by stressing the pleasures and service benefits of church association and minimizing the complexities of distinctive traditions. Believing that most Californians feel no denominational allegiance, leaders of the new churches hide their denominational ties (if they have them) with such names as Shepherd of the Hills Church, Horizon Christian Fellowship, Celebration Center, Church at Rocky Peak, Saddleback Valley Community Church. These are assumed to be more marketable names than Baptist, Lutheran, Presbyterian, Pentecostal, etc. Although the question of false advertising in order not to offend people who may feel ill-at-ease with a "denominational tag" has been raised, the rapid growth of these churches has blunted the impact of their denominational critics.

The larger question has to do with Protestant identity itself in the California environment. Community churches always have existed in the state, including independent congregations without denominational affiliation ranging from liberal to conservative orientations. Some have become large enough, such as the very conservative Grace Community Church in Burbank (with 33,000 members with 100 staff running seminary, television, and publishing programs) to be considered nearly denominations in themselves. Others, such as San Francisco's quite liberal Church for the Fellowship of All Peoples, founded in 1944 by Presbyterian Alfred G. Fisk and "a few deeply concerned persons of various races and faiths" and pastored until 1953 by the famous black Baptist social-mystic preacher and author, Howard Thurman, struggle for survival in the post-1960s religious environment. In the past, however, community churches that survived over the long haul found identity in traditions and national networks that transcended a single generation in a single geographical location.

Protestantism evolved into a world religion within distinct traditions, each modified and enriched by national, ethnic, and geographical identities. In the California environment, Protestantism's struggle for identity has thus been complicated by so many people's ambiguous attitude toward traditions and identities. A region defined since its mid-nineteenth-century U.S. statehood by continual mass migrations of peoples from other regions of the nation and the world, California has had no foundational traditions of its own into which immigrants assimilate their cultural heritages. Most Californians locate their heritage elsewhere—the U.S. East, South, or

Midwest, or countries in Europe, Asia, Africa, or Central America. If they have not come to California to escape their past and its traditions (and many have), they struggle against great odds to maintain their cultural traditions in a society that does not itself foster or nourish traditions but merely collects and envelopes them with indifference.

Yet we have seen that California Protestantism not only has survived but thrived during the past century-and-a-half. It has thrived partly on the margins of its historic denominational traditions. But it has thrived also by adapting these traditions to the California environment. It has thrived as a minority religion within a society where institutionalized religion itself encompasses less than half the population. The traditions of world religions, Protestantism included, have learned to persevere in this environment of religious innovation and plurality that does not particularly encourage or discourage any religious group, movement, or heritage. In this sense California religious history may be viewed as a foretaste of America's overall emerging religious identity, and the Protestant pilgrimage in California history may be recognized as the road being traveled by American Protestantism overall—perhaps American religion overall.

Two examples may illustrate some of the characteristics of the Protestant pilgrimage in California. These characteristics include independence in tension with denominational traditions, the liberal-conservative continuum of orientations, the continual migration of peoples into and within the state, and the racial-ethnic cultural plurality.

The Mendocino Presbyterian Church was organized in 1859—one of the first Protestant churches in California. For a century Mendocino slowly developed as a quiet community on the far northern California coast. The wooden, whitewashed Presbyterian Church building, constructed in 1869, continues to give a visual suggestion of New England to the landscape of the town, which, for nearly a century, survived economically on lumbering, fishing, and agriculture. During the 1950s the church congregation reflected the post-Second World War affluence and conventionality of most old-line Protestantism at the time.

Dramatic change came with the 1960s, and the story has been told by sociologist R. Stephen Warner in his book *New Wine in Old Wineskins: Evangelicals and Liberals in a Small-Town Church* (1988).

The cultural reach of the San Francisco metropolitan area stretched northward to Mendocino. Movie publicity attracted tourists, who in turn provided a new economic base for the community. Varieties of people began to settle in Mendocino: artists, hippies, and city folks seeking the simpler life of a small town. With them came the cosmopolitan awareness of urban society. Between 1962 and 1972 two new pastors, one of whom was Asian-American, attempted to bring vital contemporary social issues before the congregation. Each had been educated at the denomination's San Francisco Theological Seminary, a charter member in 1962 of Berkeley's ecumenical and interfaith consortium of nine Protestant and Catholic seminaries called the Graduate Theological Union. Their tireless efforts to engage the people with the upheavals of the 1960s brought tension and division within the congregation, which began to decline in membership. They also tried to reach out to the newer Mendocino residents, without much regard for Presbyterian connections, and with unforeseen consequences.

In 1969 a member of the congregation who was a committed evangelical began Antioch Fellowship as a ministry to the local counterculture. The fellowship grew to be a community of independent households, some of whom attended the Presbyterian Church, all of whom gathered weekly for Bible teaching and for informal Charismatic worship. In 1971-72 a nearby hippie commune was swept by a religious revival, and linkage was made between the commune and Antioch Fellowship. This new countercultural fellowship affected the old-line church by providing a base within the congregation to reject the liberal social activism of the 1960s in favor of more conservative evangelicalism. By 1972 the evangelicals had become a force within the congregation. They dominated the search for a new pastor that year.

The pastor chosen had graduated from Fuller Theological Seminary, the large conservative, evangelical school in Pasadena. He led the congregation in an impressive period of new growth and renewed denominational identity. Evangelicalism brought about new vitality in the church. Ironically, the renewed congregation also became a rival to Antioch Fellowship—"worldly" or "establishment" evangelicalism versus a quasi-countercultural evangelicalism. Eventually the older institution, which "could afford to be many things . . . to many people," but "presupposed that its constituents had demanding, satisfying, and salient roles elsewhere in the world," prevailed. Meanwhile, the less stable and less formal institution, which "had to be everything to its adherents," withered; denominational tradition, infused with both liberal and conservative orientations, persevered through times of social-cultural change.

About as far south as Mendocino Presbyterian Church is north on the California coast, the Los Angeles Baptist Mission Society held its annual meeting on May 4-5, 1990 at the Carson Community Center in Long Beach. Founded in 1906 by ten churches to foster mission work and start new congregations within the rapidly-growing urban environment, the Mission Society represented the mainline Northern (now American) Baptist denomination in Southern California. Within a few years mission work had begun among Spanish-speaking, Russian, Japanese, and Italian people who were settling in the greater Los Angeles area. Later, work began in the 1940s with African American black churches, and most recently (1977) with Chinese immigrants. Campus ministry programs began at the University of California at Los Angeles and at the University of Southern California in Los Angeles. By 1950 the Mission Society included 78 churches with 35,607 members.

The 1990 annual meeting of the Los Angeles Baptist Mission Society was a thoroughly multicultural event. Visibly represented on the program platform as well as among the several hundred attenders from Southern California churches were citizens of Anglo-European, African, Hispanic, and Asian heritages. Two of the three main speakers were international Baptist guests, one from Puerto Rico and the other from Korea, while the third speaker was a black pastor from a Los Angeles church. Music, language, and social-cultural interests and concerns reflected real plurality within a single Protestant denominational tradition. Calls for social justice ministries combined with "praise celebrations." The denominational seminary in distant Berkeley's Graduate Theological Union found slight visibility, overshadowed by the Baptist presence in the nondenominational Fuller Theological Seminary in nearby Pasadena.

Overall, the Los Angeles Baptist Mission Society celebrated its Southern California denominational Protestant consciousness, active within what has been described as "the most culturally complex society ever seen on the face of the earth."

SUGGESTED FURTHER READING:

Durrenberger, Robert W., ed. *California: Its People, Its Problems, Its Prospects*. Palo Alto: National Press Books, 1971.

Flowers, Ronald B. *Religion in Strange Times: The 1960s and 1970s*. Macon, Ga.: Mercer University Press, 1984.

Glock, Charles Y., and Bellah, Robert N., eds. *The New Religious Consciousness*. Berkeley: University of California Press, 1976.

Jorstad, Erling. *Holding Fast/Pressing On: Religion in America in the 1980s*. New York: Praeger, 1990.

Lewis, James R. and Melton, J. Gordon, eds. *Perspectives on the New Age*. Albany: State University of New York Press, 1992.

Marsden, George M., ed. *Evangelicalism and Modern America*. Grand Rapids, Mich.: Eerdmans, 1984.

Michaelsen, Robert S. and Roof, Wade Clark, eds. *Liberal Protestantism*. New York: The Pilgrim Press, 1986.

Quebedeaux, Richard. *The New Charismatics*. San Francisco: Harper & Row, 1983.

Roof, Wade Clark and McKinney, William. *American Mainline Religion: Its Changing Shape and Future*. New Brunswick: Rutgers University Press, 1987.

Stringfellow, William and Towne, Anthony. *The Death and Life of Bishop Pike*. Garden City, N.Y.: Doubleday, 1976.

Tipton, Steven M. *Getting Saved from the Sixties*. Berkeley: University of California Press, 1982.

Warner, R. Stephen. *New Wine in Old Wineskins: Evangelicals and Liberals in a Small-Town Church*. Berkeley: University of California Press, 1988.

Wilmore, Gayraud S., and Cone, James H., eds. *Black Theology: a Documentary History, 1966-1979*. Maryknoll, N.Y.: Orbis Books, 1979.

Wuthnow, Robert. *The Restructuring of American Religion: Society and Faith Since World War II*. Princeton: Princeton University Press, 1988.

Zikmund, Barbara Brown. "Women and the churches," chapter 7 in David W. Lotz, ed., *Altered Landscapes: Christianity in America, 1935-1985*. Grand Rapids, Mich.: William B. Eerdmans Publishing Company, 1989.

Bibliography

Learning about California's Protestants requires familiarity with both California and Protestant historiography. These two vast bodies of literature, however, have remarkably little reference to each other. California seldom appears in histories of American Protestantism, and Protestantism likewise is absent from most California histories. Notable exceptions to this exclusion in recent California historiography include, for example, Kevin Starr's *Americans and the California Dream 1850-1915* (New York: Oxford University Press, 1973), and James N. Gregory's *American Exodus: The Dust Bowl Migration and Okie Culture in California* (New York: Oxford University Press, 1989). On California historiography see Gerald D. Nash, "California and Its Historians: An Appraisal of the Histories of the State," *Pacific Historical Review* 50 (1981). Whereas many specialized accounts of particular denominations and topics of Protestant life and thought in California provide a wealth of information (see the "Protestantism in California" list below), the following works on California and on Protestantism provide a social context and religious framework for the story.

California

General Histories

Bean, Walton, and Rawls, James, Jr. *California: An Interpretive History.* New York: McGraw Hill Book Co., 1988.

Caughey, John Walton, with Hundley, Norris. *California: History of a Remarkable State.* Englewood Cliff, N.Y.: Prentice-Hall, 1982.

Lavender, David. *California: Land of New Beginnings.* Lincoln, Neb.: University of Nebraska Press, 1987.

McWilliams, Carey. *California: The Great Exception.* New York: Current Books, 1949.

Rolle, Andrew F. *California: A History.* Arlington Heights, Ill.: H. Davidson, 1987.

Watkins, T. H. *California: An Illustrated History.* New York: American Legacy Press, 1983.

Topics and Periods

Camarillo, Albert. *Chicanos in California: A History of Mexican Americans in California.* San Francisco: Boyd & Fraser, 1984.

Durrenberger, Robert W., ed. *California: Its People, Its Problems, Its Prospects.* Palo Alto: National Press Books, 1971.

Fogelson, Robert M. *The Fragmented Metropolis: Los Angeles, 1850-1930.* Cambridge: Harvard University Press, 1967.

Gregory, James N. *American Exodus: The Dust Bowl Migrations and Okie Culture in California.* New York: Oxford University Press, 1989.

Jurmain, Claudia and Rawls, James J., eds. *California: A Place, a People, a Dream.* San Francisco: Chronicle Books, 1986.

Lantis, David W., Steiner, Rodney, and Karinen, Arthur E. *California, Land of Contrast.* Dubuque, Iowa: Kendall/Hunt, 1981.

Lapp, Rudolph. *Afro-Americans in California.* San Francisco: Boyd and Fraser, 1987.

Lewis, Oscar. *San Francisco: Mission to Metropolis.* San Diego: Howell-North Books, 1980.

McGloin, John Bernard, S.J. *San Francisco: The Story of a City.* San Rafael, Ca.: Presidio Press, 1978.

Mowry, George E. *The California Progressives.* Berkeley: University of California Press, 1951.

McWilliams, Carey. *Southern California Country, An Island on the Land.* New York: Duell, Sloan & Pearce, 1946.

Nadeau, Remi. *California: The New Society.* New York: D. McKay Co., 1963.

Nash, Gerald D. *The American West Transformed: The Impact of the Second World War.* Bloomington, Ind.: Indiana University Press, 1985.

Pitt, Leonard. *Decline of the Californios: A Social History of the Spanish-Speaking Californian, 1846-1890.* Berkeley: University of California Press, 1966.

Rand, Christopher. *Los Angeles: The Ultimate City.* New York: Oxford University Press, 1967.

Rischin, Moses. "Immigration, Migration and Minorities in California," in

George H. Knoles, ed., *Essays and Assays: California History Reappraised.* Los Angeles: Ward Ritchie Press/California Historical Society, 1973.

Starr, Kevin. *Americans and the California Dream, 1850-1915.* New York: Oxford University Press, 1985.

___. *Inventing the Dream: California Through the Progressive Era.* New York: Oxford University Press, 1985.

Takaki, Ronald. *Strangers from a Different Shore: A History of Asian Americans.* Boston: Little, Brown and Company, 1989.

Wollenberg, Charles, ed. *Ethnic Conflict in California History.* Berkeley: Tinnon-Brown, 1970.

___. *Golden Gate Metropolis: Perspectives on Bay Area History.* Berkeley: Institute of Governmental Studies, University of California, 1985.

Protestantism

Brown, Robert McAfee. *The Spirit of Protestantism.* New York: Oxford University Press, 1961.

Cobb, John B., Jr. *Varieties of Protestantism.* Philadelphia: The Westminster Press, 1960.

Dillenberger, John, and Welch, Claude. *Protestant Christianity.* New York: Macmillan, 1988.

Marty, Martin. *Protestantism.* Garden City, N.Y.: Doubleday, Image Books, 1974.

Rausch, David A., and Voss, Carl Hermann. *Protestantism—Its Modern Meaning.* Philadelphia: Fortress Press, 1987.

von Rohr, John. *Profile of Protestantism.* Belmont, Ca.: Dickenson Publishing Company, Inc., 1969.

American Protestantism

Ahlstrom, Sydney E., ed. *Theology in America: The Major Protestant Voices from Puritanism to Neo-Orthodoxy.* Indianapolis: The Bobbs-Merril Company, Inc., 1967.

Brauer, Jerald C. *Protestantism In America: A Narrative History.* Philadelphia: The Westminster Press, 1974.

Clebsch, William A. *From Sacred to Profane America: The Role of Religion In American History.* New York: Harper & Row, 1968.

Ernst, Eldon G. *Without Help Or Hindrance: Religious Identity in American Culture.* Lanham, Md.: University Press of America, 1987.

Handy, Robert T. *A Christian America: Protestant Hopes and Historical Realities.* New York: Oxford University Press, 1984.

Hudson, Winthrop S. *American Protestantism.* Chicago: University of Chicago Press, 1961.

Keller, Rosemary Skinner. "Women and Religion," in Charles H. Lippy and Peter W. Williams, eds., *Encyclopedia of the American Religious Experience: Studies of Traditions and Movements.* New York: Charles Scribner's Sons, 1988.

Lincoln, C. Eric, and Mamiya, Lawrence H. *The Black Church in the African American Experience.* Durham, N.C.: Duke University Press, 1990.

Marsden, George M. *Religion and American Culture.* New York: Harcourt Brace Jovanovich, 1990.

Marty, Martin E. *Righteous Empire: The Protestant Experience in America.* New York: The Dial Press, 1970.

Mead, Sidney E. *The Lively Experiment: The Shaping of Christianity in America.* New York: Harper & Row, Publishers, 1963.

McLoughlin, William G. *Revivals, Awakenings, and Reform: An Essay on Religion and Social Change in America, 1607-1977.* Chicago: University of Chicago Press, 1978.

Niebuhr, H. Richard. *The Kingdom of God in America.* Chicago: Willett, Clark & Company, 1937.

___. *The Social Sources of Denominationalism.* New York: Henry Holt & Co., 1929.

Sylvest, Edwin, Jr. "Hispanic American Protestantism in the United States," in Moises Sandoval, ed., *Fronteras: A History of the Latin American Church in the USA Since 1513.* San Antonio, Texas: Mexican Cultural Center, 1983.

Wilmore, Gayraud S. *Black Religion and Black Radicalism: An Interpretation of the Religious History of Afro-American People.* Maryknoll, N.Y.: Orbis Books, 1983.

Region and Religion

Brauer, Jerald C. "Regionalism and Religion in America." *Church History* 54 (1985): 366-78.

Ernst, Eldon G. "American Religious History from a Pacific Coast Perspective," in Carl Guarneri and David Alvarez, eds., *Religion and Society In The American West: Historical Essays.* Lanham, Md.: University Press of America, 1987.

Gaustad, Edwin S. "Regionalism in American Religion," in *Religion in the South*, Charles Reagan Wilson, ed. Jackson: University Press of Mississippi, 1985.

Hammond, Phillip E. *Religion and Personal Autonomy: The Third Disestablishment in America.* Columbia, S.C.: University of South Carolina Press, 1992.

Hill, Samuel S. "Religion and Region in America." *The Annals of the American Academy of Political and Social Science* 480 (1985): 132-41.

Quinn, Michael D. "Religion in the American West," in *Under an Open Sky: Rethinking America's Western Past*, William Cronon, George Miles, and Jay Gitlin, eds. New York: W. W. Norton & Company, 1992.

Shortridge, James R. "A New Regionalization of American Religion," *Journal for the Scientific Study of Religion* 16 (1977): 143-54.

Sopher, David E. "Geography and Religion," *Progress in Human Geography* 5 (1981): 510-24.

Stump, Roger W. "Regional Variations in the Determinants of Religious Participation," *Review of Religious Research* 27 (1986): 208-25.

Wentz, Richard E. "Region and Religion in America," *Foundations* 24 (1981): 148-56.

Protestantism in California

Resources for the comprehensive history of California Protestantism, a story yet untold, are numerous in both unpublished and published forms. However, there are no major collections of primary sources for the broad scope of California Protestant life and thought. Small repositories of denominational church materials are scattered about the state, concentrated mostly in educational institutions located in the San Francisco-Berkeley Bay Area and in the greater Los Angeles Area. Most existing church records probably remain in the churches themselves. See Eldon G. Ernst, "Archival Sources for the History of Religion In California, Part III: Protestant Sources," *Southern California Quarterly* (Winter, 1990): 373-91; and "Churches on the United States Pacific Coast—Historical Resources," in Betty A. O'Brian, editor, *Summary of Proceedings: Forty-first Annual Conference of the American Theological Library Association* (St. Meinrad, Indiana: ATLA, 1987).

In addition to archives, over the years many published articles, books and pamphlets, plus unpublished Ph.D. dissertations and M.A. theses that treat denominational histories, regional and topical themes, and biographical topics help piece the larger story together. See Richard W. Etulain, compiler, *Religion in the Twentieth-Century American West: A Bibliography* (Albuquerque, New Mexico: Center for the American West, University of New Mexico, 1991); and Douglas Firth Anderson, "California Protestantism, 1848-1935: Historiographical Explorations and Regional Method for a Nascent Field," unpublished typescript manuscript, Graduate Theological Union Library, 1983.

The first place to turn for statistics on religion in America, including California, is Edwin Scott Gaustad, *Historical Atlas of Religion in America* (New York: Harper & Row, 1976). Other sources include Bernard Quinn, et al, *Churches and Church Membership in the United States 1980* (Atlanta: Glenmary Research Center, 1982); and George Gallup, Jr., and Jim Castelli, *The People's Religion: American Faith in the 90's* (New York: MacMillan Publishing Company, 1989). Valuable data on early twentieth-century California Protestantism is contained in *California Church Survey*, published in 1919 by the California Church Federation; and in 1945 the Federal Council of Churches, under the direction of Paul H. Douglas, published a series of statistical studies of churches in major United States urban centers, including Los Angeles and San Francisco.

Following is a selection of books, articles, dissertations and theses that treat various aspects of Protestantism in California.

Albrecht, Rudy. *The YMCA on the Western Frontier: A Brief History of the California State Young Men's Christian Association.* Los Angeles: n.p., 1964.

Anderson, Douglas Firth. "The Reverend J. Stitt Wilson and Christian Socialism in California." In Carl Guarneri and David Alvarez, editors. *Religion and Society In The American West: Historical Essays.* Lanham, Md.: University Press of America, 1987.

___. "San Francisco Evangelicalism, Regional Religious Identity, and the Revivalism of D. L. Moody." *Fides et Historia* 15 (1983): 44-56.

___. "Through Fire and Fair by the Golden Gate: Progressive Era Protestantism and Regional Culture." Ph.D. dissertation, Graduate Theological Union, 1988.

Anthony, C. V. *Fifty Years of Methodism: A History of the Methodist Episcopal Church Within The Bounds of the California Annual Conference from 1847 to 1897.* San Francisco: Methodist Book Concern, 1901.

Baird, Jesse Hays. *The San Anselmo Story: A Personalized History of San Francisco Theological Seminary.* Stockton: California Lantern Press, 1963.

Belgum, Gerhard L. "Lutherans and Rightists In California." *Lutheran Quarterly* 18 (1966): 227-34.

Bell, H. H. *A Modern Task, or the Story of the Religious Activities of the Committee of One Hundred.* San Francisco, 1916.

Birchard, Roy. "Metropolitan Community Church: Its Development and Significance." *Foundations* 20 (1977): 127-32.

Bohme, Frederick G. ""Episcopal Beginnings in Southern California." *Southern California Quarterly* 47 (1965): 171-90.

Brackenridge, R. Douglas, and Garcia-Treto, Francisco O. *Iglesia Presbiteriano: A History of Presbyterians and Mexican Americans in the Southwest.* San Antonio: Trinity University Press, 1974.

Brunner, Edmund De S. and Mary V. *Irrigation and Religion: A Study of Religious and Social Conditions in Two California Counties.* New York: George H. Doran, 1922.

Buckham, John Wright, and Charles Sumner Nash, eds. *Religious Progress on the Pacific Slope.* Boston: Pilgrim Press, 1917.

Cole, Clifford A. *The Christian Churches (Disciples of Christ) of Southern California: A History.* St. Louis: State Convention of Christian Churches, 1959.

Crompton, Arnold. *Unitarianism on the Pacific Coast: The First Sixty Years.* Boston: Beacon Press, 1957.

Douglas, H. Paul, et al. *The San Francisco Bay Area Church Study.* San Francisco: S.F. Council of Churches, 1945.

Drury, Clifford M. *A Chronology of Protestant Beginnings in California.* San Francisco: The Centennial Committee of the Northern California-Western Nevada Council of Churches, 1948.

___. "Church-Sponsored Schools in Early California." *Pacific Historian* 20 (1946): 158-66.

___. *San Francisco Y.M.C.A., One Hundred Years by the Golden Gate, 1853-1953.* Glendale: Arthur H. Clarke, 1963.

Du Brau, Richard T. *The Romance of Lutheranism In California.* St. Louis: Concordia Publishing House, 1959.

Edmondson, William Douglas. "Fundamentalist Sects of Los Angeles, 1900-1930." Ph.D. dissertation, Claremont Graduate School, 1969.

Edwards, Vina Howland. *The Story of the San Francisco Presbyterial Society, 1883-1933.* Oakland: A. Newman, 1933.

Engh, Michael Eric, S.J. *Frontier Faiths: Church, Temple, and Synagogue in Los Angeles, 1846-1888.* Albuquerque: University of New Mexico Press, 1992.

Engle, Irvin A. *Men Who Dug for Gold and Men Who Preached for God.* N.p.: Commission of Archives and History, California-Nevada Conference, United Methodist Church, 1973.

Epley, Lloyd L., ed. *Seventy-Five Years for the Kingdom: A History of California Conference United Brethren in Christ, 1864-1940.* Los Angeles: California Conference, United Brethren in Christ, 1940.

Ernst, Eldon G. "Religion in California." *Pacific Theological Review* XIX (1986): 43-51.

Ferrier, William Warren. *Congregationalism's Place In California History.* Berkeley: n.p., 1943.

___. *Pioneer Church Beginnings and Educational Movements In California.* Berkeley: n.p., 1927.

Fleming, Sanford. *For the Making of Ministers: A History of Berkeley Baptist Divinity School 1871-1961.* Valley Forge, Pa.: Judson Press, 1963.

___. *God's Gold: The Story of Baptist Beginnings in California, 1849-1860.* Philadelphia: Judson Press, 1949.

Frankiel, Sandra Sizer. *California's Spiritual Frontiers: Religious Alternatives to Anglo-Protestantism, 1850-1910.* Berkeley: Univ. of California Press, 1988.

Gilchrist, Hugh W. *A Survey of Evangelical Churches in San Francisco, Oakland, Berkeley and Alameda.* N.p.,1916.

Glock, Charles Y. and Bellah, Robert N. *The New Religious Consciousness.* Berkeley: University of California Press, 1976.

Goldschmidt, Walter R. "Class Denominationalism in Rural California Churches." *American Journal of Sociology* 49 (1944): 348-55.

Grivas, Theodore. "A History of the Los Angeles Young Men's Christian Association: The First Twenty Years." *California Historical Society Quarterly* 44 (1965): 205-227.

Hamilton, Robert S., Jr. "The History and Influence of the Baptist Church in California, 1849-1899." Ph.D. dissertation, University of Southern California, 1953.

Harvey, Sam Allen. "The Roots of California Southern Baptists, 1890-1940." S.T.D. thesis, Golden Gate Baptist Theological Seminary, 1973.

Haskell, George W. *The California Story of Congregationalism.* San Bernardino: N.p., 1961.

Haussler, John Cecil. "The History of the Seventh-day Adventist Church in California." Ph.D. dissertation, University of Southern California, 1945.

Hayashi, Brian Masaru. "'For the Sake of Our Japanese Brethren': Assimilation, Nationalism, and Protestantism Among the Japanese of Los Angeles, 1895-1942." Ph.D. dissertation, University of California, Los Angeles, 1990.

Hayashi, Brian Masaru. "The Untold Story of Nikkei Baptists in Southern California, 1913-1924." *Foundations* 22 (1979): 324-51.

Heinz, Donald. "Jesus In Berkeley." Ph.D. dissertation, Graduate Theological Union, 1976.

Helton, Helen E., and Leach, Norman E., eds. *Heritage and Hope: A History of the Protestant, Anglican and Orthodox Movement in San Francisco on the Occasion of the 75th Anniversary Year (1978-1979) of the San Francisco Council of Churches.* San Francisco: San Francisco Council of Churches, 1979.

Hine, Leland D. *Baptists in Southern California.* Valley Forge: Judson Press, 1966.

Hogue, Harland E. *Christian Seed in Western Soil: Pacific School of Religion Through a Century.* Berkeley: Pacific School of Religion, 1965.

___. "A History of Religion in Southern California, 1846-1880." Ph.D. dissertation, Columbia University, 1958.

Holland, Clifton L. *The Religious Dimension In Hispanic Los Angeles: A Protestant Case Study.* South Pasadena: William Carey Library, 1974.

Hunt, Marie Alberdina. "Chinese Christianity In California." M.A. thesis, Berkeley Baptist Divinity School, 1943.

Hurley, Mark J. *Church-State Relationships in Education in California.* Washington, D.C.: Catholic University of America, 1948.

Janzen, Kenneth L. "The Transformation of the New England Religious Tradition in California, 1849-1969." Ph.D. dissertation, Claremont Graduate School, 1964.

Jeffrey, Ernest M. "Early Religious Publications on the Pacific Coast from 1840 to 1880." B.D. thesis, San Francisco Theological Seminary, 1944.

Jervey, Edward Drewry. *The History of Methodism in Southern California and Arizona.* Nashville: The Parthenon Press, 1960.

Johnson, Margaret Waldraven. *Our Methodist Pioneers: Historical Sketches of the Beginning of the Methodist Episcopal Church, South, on the Pacific Coast.* Berkeley: California Advertising Service, 1938.

Kelley, D. O. *History of the Diocese of California from 1849 to 1914.* San Francisco: Bureau of Information and Supply, 1915.

Kip, William I. *A California Pilgrimage.* Fresno: 1921.

Koga, Sumio, compiler. *A Centennial Legacy—History of the Japanese Christian Missions in North America 1877-1977.* Chicago: Nobart, Inc., 1977.

LeShane, David Charles. *Quakers in California: The Effects of Nineteenth Century Revivalism on Western Quakerism.* Newberg: Barclay Press, 1969.

Limbaugh, Ronald H. "The Nature of John Muir's Religion." *Pacific Historian* 29 (1985): 16-29.

Loofbourow, Leon L. *In Search of God's Gold: A Story of Continued Christian Pioneering in California.* San Francisco: Historical Society of the California-Nevada Annual Conference of the Methodist Church, 1950.

___. *Cross in the Sunset: The Development of Methodism in the California-Nevada Annual Conference and of its Predecessors with Roster of all Members of the Conference.* 2 vols. San Francisco: Historical Society of the California-Nevada Conference of the Methodist Church, 1966.

Looney, Floyd. *History of California Southern Baptists.* Fresno: n.p., 1954.

Lothrop, Gloria Ricci. "West of Eden: Pioneer Media Evangelist Aimee Semple McPherson in Los Angeles." *Journal of the West* 27 (1988): 50-59.

Luckingham, Bradford. "Religion in Early San Francisco," *Pacific Historian* 17 (1973): 56-74.

Marsden, George. *Reforming Fundamentalism: Fuller Seminary and the New Evangelicalism.* Grand Rapids: Eerdmans, 1987.

McCumber, Harold O. *The Advent Message in the Golden West.* Mountain View: Pacific Press Publishing Association, 1968.

Mickler, Michael Lawrence. "James A. Pike, Bishop and Iconoclast." Ph.D. dissertation, Graduate Theological Union, 1989.

Mondello, Salvatore. "The Integration of Japanese Baptists in American Society," *Foundations* 20 (1977): 254-63.

Montesano, Philip M. "San Francisco Black Churches in the Early 1860s: Political Pressure Group." *California Historical Quarterly* 52 (1973): 145-52.

Moore, Kenneth. "Areas of Impact of Protestantism upon the Cultural Development of Northern California, 1850-1870." M.A. thesis, Pacific School of Religion, 1970.

Murphy, Larry G. "Equality Before the Law: The Struggle of Nineteenth Century Black Californians for Social and Political Justice." Ph.D. dissertation, Graduate Theological Union, 1973.

Nelson, Ronald R. "The Legal Relationship of Church and State In California." *Southern California Quarterly* 46 (1964): 11-53, 125-160.

Norton, Wesley. "Like a Thousand Preachers Flying: Religious Newspapers on the Pacific Coast to 1865." *California Historical Quarterly* 56 (1977): 194-209.

Parson, Edward Lambe. *The Diocese of California: A Quarter Century 1915-1940.* Austin, Texas: Church Historical Society, 1958.

Peters, William Bennett. "The Varieties of Religious Experience in Los Angeles, 1920-1950." Ph.D. dissertation, University of California, Santa Barbara, 1973.

Pond, William C. *Gospel Pioneering: Reminiscences of Early Congregationalism in California, 1833-1920.* Oberlin: News Printing, 1921.

Ridout, Lionel. "Foundation of the Episcopal Church in the Diocese of California, 1849-1893." Ph.D. dissertation, University of Southern California, 1953.

Seager, Robert II. "Some Denominational Reactions to Chinese Immigration to California, 1856-1892." *Pacific Historical Review* 28 (1959): 49-66.

Shelford, Paul K. *Protestant Cooperation in Northern California: The Historical Background of the Federation and Counciliar Movement.* San Francisco: Northern California-Nevada Council of Churches, 1962.

Shim, Steve Sangkwon. *Korean Immigrant Churches Today In Southern California.* San Francisco: Rand E. Research Associates, 1977.

Singleton, Gregory H. *Religion In The City of Angels: American Protestant Culture and Urbanization, Los Angeles, 1850-1930.* N.p.: UMI Research Press, 1979.

Smith, S. Raynor, Jr. "The Attitudes and Practices of the Methodist Church in California with Reference to Certain Social Crises, 1847 through 1949." Ph.D. dissertation, University of Southern California, 1955.

Stelmach, Harlan Douglas. "The Cult of Liberation: The Berkeley Free Church and the Radical Church Movement 1967-1972." Ph.D. dissertation, Graduate Theological Union, 1977.

Stensrud, E. M. *The Lutheran Church and California*. San Francisco: Trinity English Evangelical Lutheran Church, 1916.

Thacker, Ernest W. "The Methodist Church in Southern California in Relation to the Social Gospel 1928 through 1941." Ph.D. dissertation, University of Southern California, 1952.

Vasquez, Jane Atkins, ed. *Hispanic Presbyterians in Southern California: One Hundred Years of Ministry*. N.p.: Church Press, 1988.

Ware, E. B. *History of the Disciples of Christ in California*. Healdsburg: N.p., 1916.

Warner, R. Stephen. *New Wine in Old Wineskins: Evangelicals and Liberals in a Small-Town Church*. Berkeley: University of California Press, 1988.

Washburn, James F. *History and Reminiscences of Holiness Church Work in Southern California and Arizona*. South Pasadena: n.p., 1910.

Watkins, Walter F. *The Cry of the West: The Story of the Mighty Struggle for Religious Freedom in California*. San Francisco: R&E Research Associates, 1969.

Weber, Francis J., ed. *The Religious Heritage of Southern California: A Bicentennial Survey*. Los Angeles: Interreligious Council of Southern California, 1976.

Whitaker, Robert. "Is California Irreligious?" *Sunset Magazine* 16 (1906): 382-85.

Wicher, Edward Arthur. *The Presbyterian Church In California 1849-1927*. New York: The Grafton Press, 1927.

___. *A Summary of the History of San Francisco Theological Seminary*. San Anselmo, Ca., 1921.

Willard, Ruth Hendricks, Wilson, Carol Green, and Flamm, Roy, *Sacred Places of San Francisco*. Novato, Ca.: Presidio Press, 1985.

Woo, Wesley S. "Protestant Work Among the Chinese in the San Francisco Bay Area, 1850-1920." Ph.D. dissertation, Graduate Theological Union, 1983.

Woods, Betty. "An Historical Survey of the Woman's Christian Temperance Union of Southern California." M.A. thesis, Occidental College, 1950.

Yoshida, Ryo. "A Socio-Historical Study of Racial Ethnic Identity In the Inculturated Religious Expression of Japanese Christianity in San Francisco 1877-1924." Ph.D. dissertation, Graduate Theological Union, 1989.

Index